D0965958

Escape from Empire

Escape from Empire

The Developing World's Journey through Heaven and Hell

Alice H. Amsden

The MIT Press
Cambridge, Massachusetts
London, England

MIT Press books may be purchased at special quantity discounts for business or sales promotional use. For information, please email special_sales@mitpress.mit.edu or write to Special Sales Department, The MIT Press, 55 Hayward Street, Cambridge, MA 02142.

This book was set in Stone Serif and Stone Sans on 3B2 by Asco Typesetters, Hong Kong, and was printed and bound in the United States of America.

Library of Congress Cataloging-in-Publication Data

Amsden, Alice H. (Alice Hoffenberg)
Escape from empire : the developing world's journey through heaven and hell / Alice H. Amsden.
p. cm.
Includes bibliographical references (p.) and index.
ISBN-13: 978-0-262-01234-8 (hardcover : alk. paper)
1. Developing countries—Foreign economic relations—United States. 2. United States—Foreign economic relations—Developing countries. 3. Developing countries—Economic conditions. I. Title.
HF1413.A48 2007
337.730172′4—dc22 2006033363

10 9 8 7 6 5 4 3 2 1

Contents

Acknowledgments

The idea presented in this book is a hot potato because it turns the meaning of laissez-faire on its head: instead of free markets, laissez-faire signifies free developing economies. Freedom is truest when the great powers let the developing world chart its own economic course and choose its own mix of market and state, as done to a tee by the fastest-growing late developers.

For whatever reasons, debates over American foreign economic policy usually end in rage. Few subjects seem capable of creating such emotion. Special thanks are thus due to readers of early drafts of this book, who page by page may have gritted their teeth. Lonnie Edelheit, second-in-command of General Electric under Jack Welch, staked out one very useful critique. Duncan Kennedy, originator of critical legal studies at Harvard Law School, staked out another. But all readers had interesting things to say in a multitude of directions, including Goolam Aboobaker, Judith Aptekar, Wan-wen Chu, Salo Vinocur Coslovsky, Cui Zhiyuan, Carter Eckert, João Carlos Ferraz, the late Andre Gunder Frank, David Friend, Marvin Gettleman, Takashi Hikino, Alan Hirsch, Charlotte Hlongwane, Rolph van der Hoeven, Helga Hoffmann, Ayman Ismail, Calestous Juma, Maryellen Kelley, Lex Kelso, Duncan Kincaid, Yevgeny Kuznetsov, Daniel Malkin, Karuna Murdaya, Patrick K. O'Brien, José Antonio Ocampo, Tom Reinhart, Arthur Schlesinger, Margaret Shephard, Ajit Singh, Andrés Solimano, Myra Strober, Lance Taylor, Elliott Thrasher, and David Unger.

The potato is now out of the oven and, ideally, is tasty to everyone.

From Heaven to Hell

1 Heaven Can't Wait

There were giants in the Earth in those days.
Genesis 6:4

I Eagle Eyes

For more than half a century after World War II, first one American empire and then another dominated a territory larger than that imagined by King Solomon or Alexander the Great. The first lifted all boats; the second lifted all yachts. In one case, prosperity and growth were graced by Heaven. In the other, inequality and stagnation were squired by Hell. Whatever we can say about the rise and fall of American imperialism, it was not black or white, and it saw big changes. The new economic stars that are now forming in the firmament, constellations like China and India, will rapidly alter survival patterns here on earth.

Under the First American Empire, from 1950 to 1980, the world enjoyed an economic Golden Age. Growth in developing countries, whether Africa or the Middle East, soared. Nothing comparable had occurred before, nor has there been anything comparable since. The average growth in national income and income per head may have been faster than in any stage of colonial history. In terms of the betterment of its subjects, the First American Empire can take a deep bow.

Then, after 30 years, it was struck by lightning. It died at the hands of war (Vietnam), oil (price hikes), and cheap credit (Wall Street). As the 1970s passed, as news went from bad to worse, the plucky, prosperous era lasting from Franklin Roosevelt to Richard Nixon came to a halt. A Second American Empire arose in 1980, with the elections of Ronald Reagan and Margaret Thatcher. Soon a debt crisis convulsed poor countries, and for at least the next 25 years the Second American Empire's orthodox medicines failed to revive them. Heaven slowly gave way to Hell. A Golden Age became enshrouded in darkness. Within influential circles, debate all but ceased, and the intellectual dimension of development grew silent. Only awesome Asia consistently moved closer to the world's technological frontier.

Whether or not an empire is morally responsible for its subjects, when they thrive, it thrives. The Second American Empire thrived all right, but its people didn't, creating a much more menacing challenge for "globalism."

The Third World's booms and busts are commonly explained as the result of its culture, because the process of modernization is always pulled and pushed by a people's history. According to one popular myth, Asia grew quickly under Confucianism because Confucius respected hard work. But Asia didn't always grow quickly, and when it grew slowly, in the 1950s, Confucianism was blamed just the same, on the grounds that Confucius held commerce in low esteem. If culture doesn't change but growth rates jump up and down, then culture is a poor predictor of growth. To make culture a meaningful predictor, its contradictions have to be taken into account. Every culture has a counterculture. One American says, "Nobody likes us." The other says, "Everybody wants to be like us, so they must love us." A culture is a set of beliefs, behavioral norms, organizations, and policies, while a counterculture is an opposite set.

The American Empire's own culture and counterculture made a deep impression on all developing countries. Cultural dominance flowed from U.S. power. After the Second World War, American per capita income and average Third World per capita income diverged, starting at a ratio of around 4:1 or 5:1 and growing, at the extreme, to around 40:1. The bigger the gap, the larger the area of imperial influence. Sometimes the influence is good for the developing world, sometimes it is a disaster.

From 1929 to 1980, an American counterculture, involving both Democratic and Republican presidents, was built on three pedestals—Knowledge, Inventiveness, and Experimentation. On top of this were the two drivers of development, Market and State. Then, balancing unevenly on these, at the very top, was American Foreign Economic Policy.

The historical root of American heterodoxy was "no ordinary time."[1] It starts with the fall from grace of free enterprise for its ignoble role in the Great Depression, followed by Keynes's economic experiment, the New Deal's attempt at industrial planning, wartime mobilization and demobilization, the red revolution, the Green Revolution, and the electronics revolution. President Kennedy's close assistant and Pulitzer Prize–winning historian, Arthur Schlesinger Jr., described the United States as "a country for experiment." From all this came the greatest gift of the United States to the Third World—"use your own brains and run your own show." This version of laissez-faire might be summed up in the words of President Richard Nixon: "Nobody gave a damn."

Still, however golden an age, however experimental a generation's mindset, even the savants make stupendous mistakes. The Soviet Union was regarded as a tiger when, in reality, it was a paper tiger, while Vietnam was regarded as a paper tiger when, in reality, it was a tiger. The Cold War against the Soviets consumed billions of dollars and the Third World got almost nothing, not even when it tried to play Moscow and Washington off against each other. The one plum was Egypt's Aswan Dam. The war in Vietnam was catastrophic because the United States didn't know how to fight a people's war; the same happened again in the war in Iraq. America lacked the information, know-how, and experimentation it swore by, and without these it fell.

The Second American Empire arose on the embers of Vietnam and the hot coals of Japanese competition. If the motto of the First Empire was "Get smart," then the motto of the Second Empire was "Get tough." Financial services were becoming the largest single industry in the United States. To spread its wings, Wall Street demanded that the Treasury Department get Third World countries to deregulate their financial markets. No less vocal, multinationals wanted developing countries to practice free trade and drop all investment controls. Both Republican and Democratic presidents heard their pleas. Experimentation became cynical, as it had been under the British Empire; as J. V. Puryear writes, "In the early nineteenth century, the principle of free trade was introduced by the British into Turkey before it was accepted in Great Britain."[2] The Second American Empire first tried globalism in the developing countries before their sugar, rice, corn, and cotton could enter U.S. markets duty-free. As the Southern Hemisphere liberalized its manufacturing sector, the United States continued to protect its own manufacturers against Third World's specialties—machine tools, textiles, and steel. When financial markets crashed, deregulation had yet to be tested to see if it worked, but despite the desperation of millions of people, the United States never changed course.

A 1998 report by a Clinton appointee, the U.S. Trade Representative, conveys the demons behind deregulating and dismantling the state: "It is vital to the long-term prosperity and prestige of the United States...to take full advantage of our strong global position and *continue to push our trading partners for even more open markets and economic liberalization*. If we abdicate our strength, we risk missing a prime opportunity to advance those policies and values that have been so instrumental in making our economy the strongest and most efficient in the world."[3] This tough talk, a Hollywood version of the great economists Ricardo and Smith, takes for granted the win-win plot of the movies. The world's most competitive economies can tough out imports and thrive when weaker markets are opened. They have everything to gain from free trade. In theory, openness also helps the weak, despite the danger that imports will crush their infant industries. Instead, poor countries are saved by foreign investors. The industries of poor countries are built *and owned* by foreign investors. The market knows no ownership, but developing countries do not have everything to gain from liberalizing first.

After World War II, America's hippie counterculture, with its experimentation, outperformed America's orthodox culture, with its market mantras. *Why the unexpected performance of the two empires, especially since both are cut from the same cloth*? And why was Asia, alone among developing regions, blessed twice, growing rapidly no matter who was in power?

The sleuth that stars in this study, the author, sets out to solve these mysteries of economic life.

II The Book of Numbers

How convincing is the case presented in this book that the effect of the United States on the developing world in the twentieth century is analogous to a fall from Heaven to Hell? Are the two American empires so different? Can't their initial differences explain most of their subsequent behavior (decolonization, the rise of Asia, the fall of Latin America)?

The weaknesses of the arguments cannot be denied. Although post–World War II American imperialism can be partitioned, the First and Second Empires have more in common than meets the eye. Throughout the postwar years, the United States has been a tough guy; even Third World governments that were democracies but hostile to America's economic interests usually didn't survive for very long—witness Mossadegh in Iran in 1953, sitting on oil, and Allende in Chile in 1973, sitting on copper. For another, both empires were solicitous of American big business—part culture and part campaign donations. The First Empire was a great champion of decolonization, not least of all because it gave American industry a chance to penetrate markets previously monopolized by Britain and France. Development in both periods was dependent on massive technology transfers that were more difficult than anyone had imagined, because the expectation was widespread that Third World industrialization would be undertaken by *American* multinational firms. Markets, prices, and political control were the hallmarks of how America operated throughout the last half of the twentieth century.

Both empires lent little on soft terms to developing countries for the purpose of establishing modern industries, the heart of economic development. This stinginess undermined the effectiveness of foreign aid, although all donors tied roughly 80 percent of their aid to purchases from their own countries. Without investments in new plant and equipment to create jobs, foreign aid for water, sewage, roads, and education raised human welfare but not employment. Schooling was emphasized, but unemployed school graduates were ignored. Neither empire wanted the Third World to become a competitor.

Much more can also be said against the state interventionist model and the Third World strategy of import substitution (producing locally what was formerly imported). State intervention in many countries supposedly bred gross inefficiency and cancerous corruption. If a state picks winners, where does it get its wizardry? How can one talk about Heaven when that age harbored hippies and interventionist states?

Yet, whatever the weaknesses of the schema of two distinct epochs—one heaven-sent and the other hell-bound—all the numbers for the years after World War II strongly support it. Growth was faster, on average, under government intervention than under free markets, although, because of "retained" institutions, markets never became wildly free.[4] The most contentious market to be opened was for capital.

The striking difference in growth rates between the First and Second American Empires is shown in figure 1.1. In the Golden Age, between 1950 and 1980, income grew faster in developing countries than in developed ones—on average a little over 5 percent a year compared with 4

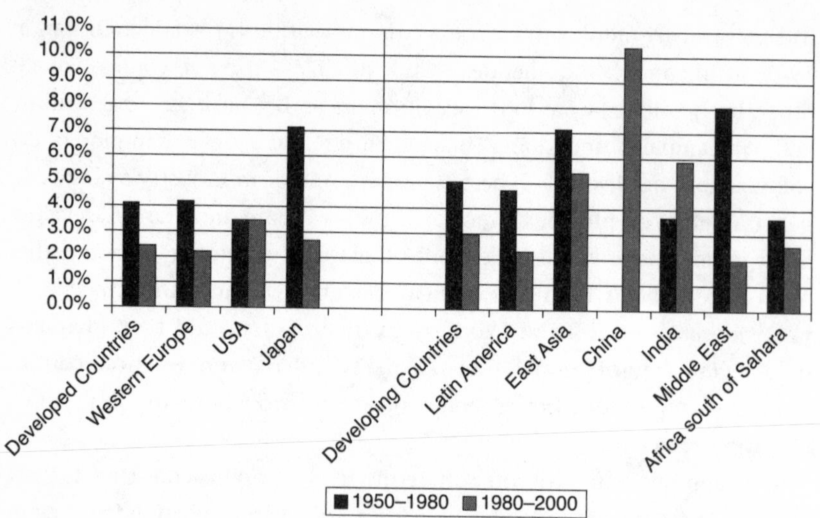

Figure 1.1
Growth in income: 1950–1980 and 1980–2000. Source: World Tables (World Bank, 1980, 1994); *World Development Report* Development Indicators (World Bank, 2002); and World Bank online data.

percent. This was a first in recorded history (according to World Bank data), a period of unprecedented expansion in living standards, per capita income, wages, and poverty reduction. Then the boom ended: inflation from rising oil prices and the Vietnam War led to monetarism at the Federal Reserve. A sharp cut in the money supply forced up interest rates on the loans developing countries had to repay, and made it more difficult for unemployed American workers to buy foreign goods. A new empire appeared with new policies. Then the average growth rates in the Third World plummeted and barely reached 3 percent for more than 25 years. The Middle East's decline was steepest, from about 8 percent to 2 percent, as savings and investment fell. Latin America and Africa also suffered high and chronic unemployment and a sharp slowdown: "Average annual growth rates in GDP per capita in Latin America and the Caribbean went down from 3 percent in 1960–1980 to 0.5 per cent in 1980–2002."[5] Whereas Latin America's income per head grew by 10 percent in the entire 25 years from 1980 to 2005, it grew by 82 percent in the 20 years from 1960 to 1980. According to the UN's *Human Development Report* (1990), a low-income country like Kenya had reasonably good growth in the 1960s and 1970s, when its income per head rose by about 3 percent a year. But like most African countries, it suffered negative growth in the 1980s, with per capita income falling by about 0.9 percent a year. The 1990s weren't much better.

The growth rate in the United States was unique—about the same in both periods. But income distribution became more unequal, approximating the huge gap between rich and poor in Latin America. American median family income (in 1996 dollars) barely budged from $40,400 in 1973 to only $43,200 in 1996, a mere 7 percent growth *over the entire twenty-three-year period*! While the top brackets captured more wealth, this stagnant median income occurred even as many families had to send two income-earners into the labor force to make ends meet, and many workers had to hold two jobs.[6] The 99.99th percentile of Americans enjoyed a 17 percent annual increase in income, with their absolute income averaging about $6 million a year![7] Something similar happened in Japan once it began to recover in 2005 after a long recession. There was national hand-wringing after a loss of egalitarianism which was attributed to "Reagan-esque" policies such as deregulation, privatization, spending cuts, and tax breaks for the rich.

Most economists studying developing countries have found that the more equal income distribution is, the more rapidly national income grows. How equality affects growth is unclear, and measures of equality vary, but all seem to point in the same direction. Many peasants were thrown off the land under colonialism, and land concentration led to high inequality in rural areas, where most people lived. The First American Empire started a movement in Asia toward greater equality by introducing land reform in Japan under the Supreme Commander of the Allied Forces in the Pacific, which also democratized education and decapitated the *zaibatsu*, or big business groups. In contrast, land reform fell into the dustbin of history under the Second American Empire even though huge numbers of peasants were still employed on the land. As the population shifted to urban areas, other distribution measures were studied, and most show inequality worsening. In Latin America, the share of employment in the "informal" sector rose from 52 percent to 58 percent in only seven years, from 1990 to 1997; it is better to be employed in the "formal" sector because the informal sector includes self-employed workers with very low incomes and bad working conditions. The share of national income (value added) going to wages instead of capital has also fallen: in six out of eight Latin American countries chosen for their data availability, the wage share fell. In

Mexico, the guinea pig of the "Washington consensus" (the Treasury, State Department, World Bank, and IMF), the wage share plunged from 37 percent in 1975–80 to 20 percent in 1985–92. The wage share stayed almost steady in Korea, Singapore, Indonesia, Malaysia, Thailand, and the Philippines. It fell—sometimes as much as in Mexico—in Ghana, Zimbabwe, Egypt, Morocco, Tunisia, and Turkey. Out of a sample of developing countries, real wages between 1975–1979 and 1987–1991 fell in 16 out of 24 cases. Generally the fall in equality, and wages, was greatest in Africa, Latin America, and the Middle East.[8]

Most Asian countries had very equal income distributions by world standards and a different model of capitalism from "Reaganomics" or neoliberalism. The ideology of free markets was taken with a grain of salt. The law of comparative advantage was obeyed on and off, as countries used their prewar manufacturing experience and state support to march into mid-tech industries like automobiles, petrochemicals, shipbuilding, and steel. China and India grew relatively slowly in the years immediately after World War II. Planning was too centralized in China, but the foundations of modern industry were laid, electricity reached almost all villages, education became nearly universal, and government R&D institutes accumulated human capital. India's growth rate was faster than the average growth rate after 1980 for developing countries as a whole. India grew slowly because it took time off from industrialization to become self-sufficient in food and to succor small-scale firms. Then, after market reforms, protection of the old political constituency of Gandhi—the artisan and small producer—lost ground to big business—the favorite son of Nehru, India's first prime minister. Output rose over time, soaring in the early 1990s even before market reforms began. Software services boomed in the remote region of Bangalore, which benefited from former government investments in electronics, telecommunications, aerospace, and a prestigious Indian Institute of Science. The military chose Bangalore as a center of science and technology because it was safe from Russian and Chinese attack. Soon the Bangalore region had more experienced engineers than any other part of India. When software services sprang up there, the contribution of government was invisible to the naked eye. Growth after 1978 in China was phenomenal, fueled by a 35 to 40 percent savings rate. Economic theory has never satisfactorily answered why savings rates (savings as a share of income) differ across countries, but other Asian countries also save a lot. The saving rate in India rose to roughly 30 percent, while it rose to only 20 percent or less in Latin America.

After the fall of the Berlin wall, Russia let market forces rip, and its economy collapsed. China never experienced such a catastrophe and it never entirely retired its state-run system, the founder of modern industry. China adapted the model used by Japan, Korea, Taiwan, and Thailand, which combined not just market and state, but also subsidies and performance standards. Before being eligible for soft loans, science-intensive firms had to reach certain performance standards related to investments in R&D and new product development. The high *ideal* for government was to give nothing away for free. Still, the Gini coefficient for urban China rose from 16 in 1978, when market reforms began, to 28 in 1995 (the higher the Gini, the greater the inequality).

Capital formation and poverty alleviation went hand in hand; one created capable people and one created jobs to employ them. According to the Asian Development Bank, between 1960 and 2000 Asia's rate of poverty (people living at subsistence) fell from 65 percent to 17 percent, infant mortality was down from 141 per 1,000 births to 48, and life expectancy was up from 41 years to 67.

From Washington to Wall Street, Latin America in the 1990s was expected to become the next superstar. Because it had democratized politically and it had sounded a neoconservative wake-up call, Latin America was considered a good bet by the financial community. But in Mexico, Washington's laboratory for free trade, per capita income increased on average by 3.1 percent a year between 1935 and 1982 and then by a mere 0.02 percent a year between 1983 and 1999. In the same two periods, Mexico's minimum wage first rose on average by 1.4 percent a year and then fell by 6.9 percent a year. Financial crises became a recurrent feature of the Mexican scene and in Latin America at large. In Puerto Rico, a U.S. Commonwealth, GDP in the 1940s ran like a rabbit. From 1960 to 1970 growth was almost as fast as that of Asia's island economies: Singapore, 8.8 percent; Hong Kong, 10 percent; and Taiwan, 9.2 percent. Then from 1975 to 1984, under a new banking system, Puerto Rico's GDP growth plummeted, to 1.9 percent, while Asia's held firm (8.5 percent, 9.9 percent, and 8.0 percent respectively).[9] Argentina, one of the worst fatalities of the debt fiasco, recovered in the 2000s only by ignoring the IMF's advice (the same was true of Korea after the Asian financial crisis of 1997). A report on Bolivia concluded, "the market-oriented changes that Washington long ago prescribed for Latin America have brought little or no prosperity to the average person, with some lands poorer than before."[10] Bolivia's president in 2005, Evo Morales, a former coca plantation worker, led the political party Movement toward Socialism as a way out of Bolivia's woes. Despite its discovery of natural gas, Bolivia's per capita income was lower in 2005 than 25 years earlier. The popular refrain in a Peruvian election in 2006 was "many have tired of the American-inspired free trade model." Latin American trade improved after 2000, but mainly because it started exporting raw materials to China. Catfish exports to the United States were booming in Chile, Latin America's favorite son. Few skilled, well-paying jobs were involved in either case.

The Second American Empire would ultimately incur the costs of not helping Latin America heal. Its economy sank as Asia's soared.

III Heaven Hails the Mind

Despite its much-debated spread of Western civilization, colonialism failed for the most part to increase the Third World's collective income or income per head. After the Marines took control, Washington made the Philippines a paragon of education. But despite rich natural resources and human talent, the Philippines never took off. Cuba, another American colony, was in such bad shape after 60 years of U.S. rule that it was overrun by a small band of armed guerrillas led by Fidel Castro. Even the best-case growth rates under the British Empire were shockingly low. The jewel in Britain's crown, India, saw its income grow from the mid nineteenth century to 1947 at something *just under one percent a year*. Egypt's per capita income fell by roughly 20 percent between 1900 and 1945. Nigeria's per capita income toward the end of British occupation in 1963 was officially estimated at £2, low even for the time.[11] The British Empire, not much different from the Second American Empire, is best remembered as a place where "the sun never sets and wages never rise."

Bad publicity for colonialism and its chintzy diffusion of knowledge emerged only slowly. With the hindsight of history, we can see that *all* the countries that succeeded in entering the orbit of modern world industry after World War II had acquired manufacturing experience in prewar days, some in Latin America, most under colonialism. *But very few of over 100 countries under colonialism had acquired manufacturing experience at all!* Without experience, it was hard to identify a marketable product, raise finance, build a firm, and produce to specification—all the factors of what we call entrepreneurship. Experience made it possible to guess what investments were "winners" with a reduced margin of error. Experience gave companies confidence that they could earn long-term profits, rather than make a killing through corruption. In turn, the profit-maximizing firm made it far more likely that government subsidies would be used productively. Manufacturing experience meant more effective government. But a "market" way of thinking emphasizes exchange, not production.

The great classical economists largely saw development in terms of market exchange, transactions, buying and selling, and the prices necessary to make transactions efficient. Prices are the economist's stock in trade. Knowledge about production and technology was taken as given, which is understandable since the technology of the time was virtually free. To produce pins, Adam Smith's brilliant example of the division of labor, manufacturers had only to look around and observe how pins were made; the technology was there for the having. But today, even a peeping Tom can't learn how to make a pin through sheer observation. What new materials is it made of? How does the machinery work? How are pins packaged? As big business arose and innovation became a matter of life and death, as corporate research and development laboratories became science-based and proprietary, knowledge became valuable and closely guarded. It became tacit rather than documented. The problem of development had changed, even if established wisdom hadn't.

Asian or Latin American companies, maneuvering to enter mid-tech industries like hard steel and health serums, were pressed to get the knowledge they needed to sell at minimum cost. They required new institutions to compete—to acquire, adapt, and master technology. They required state support as learning got under way, otherwise they would sink as foreign competitors "dumped" in world markets, as they leveraged their brand names and high quality, as they flexed their manufacturing muscles and marketing might. But because the Second American Empire let opening markets and "getting the prices right" crowd out acquiring technology and building institutions to exploit it, the developing world was doomed to Hell.

IV Heaven's Hippie Experiment

Whatever their shortfalls, Third World industrial policies under the First American Empire gave something to everyone: higher-paying industrial jobs to upwardly mobile workers; chances for small- and medium-sized enterprises to produce modern parts and components; employment for professional managers and engineers who had previously taken to emigrating; opportunities for the financial sector to lend to new firms; and chances for experienced entrepreneurs to make fair-sized fortunes. The idea was to industrialize by letting imports guide what was to be produced. This was safe and sound. After wartime shortages, a pent-up demand for imports exploded and endangered the balance of payments. Everyone in the tropics wanted air conditioners. Everyone wanted TVs. Everyone needed trucks or tractors, bicycles or scooters, machinery and medicines. "Import substitution" saved foreign exchange and was *demand-driven*: if something was imported, obviously locals were willing to pay for it, so the demand was there. The manufacture of TVs, for example, also enhanced technological know-how more than exporting copper and corn. Import substitution was learning-intensive. A worker on a TV assembly line was paid a pittance, but didn't have to face the dangers of a mine or back-breaking agricultural work.

But this counterculture was in violation of the law of comparative advantage, which dictates that markets be supply-driven. If a country has lots of labor, it should make only what requires a lot of labor to produce. According to a leading orthodox economist at the University of Chicago, a country can gain as much from producing potato chips as from making computer chips. Washington's advice became acerbic: "Don't produce what is imported, which might take an eon to learn and will almost certainly require protective tariffs. Produce what can already be exported, which has proven its worth. Produce more raw materials."

Comparative advantage was debunked after World War II by the United Nation's Latin American office. Raul Prebisch, an Argentine economist later vindicated by history, was the main advocate of import-substitution industrialization because he argued that prices of raw materials, which accounted for around 90 percent of Third World exports, had fallen over time relative to the prices of manufactures. Raw-material exporters had to give more and more just to stand still. They were also losing from technological change, as synthetics substituted for natural rubber; as nylon substituted for silk, hemp, and sisal; as aluminum preempted pig iron; as saccharine supplanted sugar; and so on. The First American Empire satanized Prebisch, but its objections were brushed aside. Like the hippies, the Third World dropped out of orthodoxy and won the day.

Despite all the bad press, even the most efficient mature high-tech industries now practice import substitution. In Asia, assemblers of calculators, computers, and cell phones first buy hundreds of their parts and components from overseas, mostly from Japan. Then step-by step they selectively import-substitute them. Protection never enters, but its equivalent does. The government provides assemblers with science parks, semiconductor design services, spillovers from government labs, cheap credit, and joint R&D.

Unexpectedly, import substitution in countries with manufacturing experience became the mother of mid-tech exports such as steel, cement, petrochemicals, automobiles, truck parts, TVs, and tires. An industry would start selling in the domestic market and then, with enough experience, would sell overseas. The whole idea that export-led growth and import substitution were at odds proved to be mismeasured and false.

V Root of All Evil

Japan's black magic in manufacturing in the 1980s led to a massive restructuring of American industry. The share of manufacturing in national income declined, and with it, an American way of life. Trade unions became almost extinct, and manufacturing job shops in inner cities closed their doors. The service sector rose in importance, especially financial services. This industry became the favorite of the Treasury, comprising a dense network of stock exchanges, commodity brokers, investment banks, commercial banks, savings banks, nonbank financial intermediaries, and venture capitalists. The Third World was seen as an emerging *market,* a vacuum cleaner to absorb these services, rather than as an emerging *economy*, capable of supplying some of them itself.

The rise of the financial services sector, the triumph of the Treasury over the State Department in foreign economic affairs, and the plunge in Third World growth rates are all closely connected. The causality runs something like this, in rough order: first, there is deregulation of the Third World's financial markets, starting in some countries even before World War II (the Treasury); then there is "loan pushing" to Third World borrowers (Wall Street); loan pushing leads to overborrowing to finance long-dreamed-of projects (the developing world); rising interest rates raise the costs of Third World loan repayments (the Federal Reserve); there is an outbreak of a deadly and contagious debt disease (the Third World, excluding Asia), and as a condition for raising money to repay overdue loans, the Third World must abandon state economic interventions (the Treasury, the Fed, the International Monetary Fund, and the World Bank). Because most developing countries, with a long history of prudently regulating their inflows and outflows of capital, were burned by "hot" money, this truly was Hell.

Now the Emperor has no clothes. It is undeniable that the Second American Empire's attempts to restart Third World growth have failed. Populist governments are appearing in Latin America, unemployment is destabilizing urban life in Africa and the Middle East, and religious fundamentalism is spreading throughout the world. Excluding Asia, which has faithfully followed Japan and the First American Empire's freelance approach, the engine pulling the rest of the Third World badly needs fixing.

How did a venerable culture of open markets fail to ignite development in so many countries?

VI Heaven Wears Extra-Large

While *on average* Third World growth rates in the postwar years fell from high to low, averages sometimes hide a truth. During both a Golden Age and a Dark Age, Asia rose like a phoenix. It grew and grew, with Japan as mentor, the most creative catch-up case of them all. Growth first started accelerating in East Asia, in Japan's former colonies of Korea and Taiwan. Then it spread to Southeast Asia, in countries such as Indonesia, Malaysia, and Thailand. It rose steadily in the city-states of Singapore and Hong Kong. Then it spread to South Asia, mostly India. As these countries rejected neoconservatism and orthodox laissez-faire, as they designed *unique mixtures of market and state,* their footprints became larger and larger. Soon, after a long sleep, there were giants in the earth. These were countries with low wages, huge populations, and a growing class of university students, professional managers, skilled workers, and experienced engineers. China and India awoke, having once been great empires in their own right. Brazil, Indonesia, and Iran began warming up in the wings. Southern Nigeria and South Africa were stewing in the waiting room. These were smart and precocious giants, unlike those defeated in mythical Greece.

Edward Gibbon, the great Enlightenment writer on Rome, argued in the eighteenth century that the reins of power would always reside in Europe and its offshoots because that is where new technology was born. Power would merely shift from one advanced country to another, as in the past. In contrast, Oxford historian Arnold J. Toynbee argued in his twelve-volume world history, published beginning in 1934, that in the very long run, power would flow to countries with the largest populations (and the strongest religions).[12] Some developing countries today have huge populations dating from when they were empires in their own right, and also from colonial days, when they were stitched together from independent kingdoms by European powers such as Portugal (Brazil), the United Kingdom (India), and Holland (Indonesia). Holland couldn't conquer Aceh for almost 30 years, and then in 1908 it united it with Java, Bali, Celebes, and Madura to form a single colony, named Indonesia, under Dutch rule. Ironically, colonialists were responsible for creating many of the Third World giants that later cut them down to size!

With giants in the earth, not for a long time to come will an empire reign the way the United States reigned after World War II. With the awakening of giants, *global absolute power has become a relic of the past.* Absolutism cannot be preserved by the United States, nor can it be acquired by China. No longer can a single country enjoy it. What will empower an empire now is how "great" it is, meaning how much it promotes global economic development. Otherwise, the Vietnams, Afghanistans, and Iraqs of history will keep repeating themselves, and cutting down even the strongest empire at the knees.

China is larger than life because it does not stand alone. It is part of Asia, and if Asian economies continue to gallop away, so will China's economy, and vice versa. Regional trade, regional investment, regional manufacturing, and the regional exchange of ideas, fashions, music, and movies ("soft" power) have formed an Asian bloc that can be expected to rival the American states and the European Union. As unemployment jumps from one bloc to another, national obligations to create employment will rise. But with more competition, world welfare will also rise.

Asia has been thrown together through trade ties, but it has been diplomatically divided since the dinosaurs. Korea hates Japan, Japan hates China, and so on. Still, these sorts of divisions displease a new middle class. When Condoleezza Rice, the U.S. Secretary of State under George W. Bush, sounded a "cautionary note" about conferring with China, financial analysts in the Asian region said Rice's notion seemed "passé."[13] The dawn of the Asian century has eclipsed the dreary years of internal rivalry, and now Asia is set on competing against the West.

The United States has no equivalent regional relationship. The United States is Latin America's best and worst friend. It imports almost half its oil from Latin America. American foreign investment south of the border is large, over 90 percent of Mexico's exports go to American and Canadian markets, and Latino immigrants have changed the face of American cities. After falling into debt in the 1980s, Latin America became as ideological about free markets as Washington. Latin intellectuals are as Western as New Englanders, and as strong believers in the Enlightenment as Bostonians. At the same time, anti-American sentiment persists. The legacy of the Monroe Doctrine and President Teddy Roosevelt's corollary to it—which stated that the United States, a "civilized" nation, had the right to stop "chronic wrongdoing" throughout the Western Hemisphere—still lingers. Between the end of the Spanish-American War and the Great Crash, American troops are estimated to have invaded Latin America at least 32 times. The overthrow of a popularly elected Chilean president in 1973 created widespread unrest. Following the failure of free markets to halt Latin America's economic descent, "Yankee go home!" was again heard in countries ranging from Brazil, Argentina, and Venezuela, to Uruguay, Ecuador, and Peru. But the Yanks have not gone home.

The United States should be running a trade surplus with Latin America, Latin America should be running a trade surplus with Asia, and Asia should be (and is) running a trade surplus with the United States. But the United States can't run a trade surplus with Latin America because Latin America's industries are in shambles and its imports are weak.

The rivalry between the United States and China will depend on the relative performance of Asia and Latin America. As of now, Asia is a plum and Latin America is a lemon. To do anything about this, the Second American Empire will have to become less ideological and pay Latin America its due: a modern Marshall Plan. Yet all this empire shows is an inability to change.

VII Democracy

Today's great empires no longer enjoy direct, formal political control over their subjects. Times have changed since India's Sepoy Mutiny in 1857 or China's Boxer Rebellion in 1900, when the fight waged against foreigners was a matter of liberty or death. But arguably, imperial power over the Third World today has *grown stronger* because differences in income between rich and poor countries have widened. Equating power with income, the global distribution of both has become more skewed than ever before. In the past, the per capita income of developed countries exceeded that of developing countries by a factor of four or five. Now, the gap may be as large as 30 or 40: for every dollar a poor developing country has, a developed country has 40 times more!

The developing world itself is sharply divided by income per head, with some countries (or regions within countries) being far more industrialized than others. In the beginning, countries were divided by population: dense in Asia, sparse in Africa, Latin America, and the Middle East. Foreign invaders worsened poverty in poor agricultural regions that were sparsely populated by the forceful creation of a low-wage labor force. Instead of obeying market rules and paying high wages for scarce labor to work in the gold, copper, and diamond mines of southern Africa, or the coffee, tea, and sisal estates of Kenya, colonialists concocted excuses to take away people's land, forcing them into paid employment at a pittance. Africans had no alternative means of support. Force was the origin of a low-wage economy in what were initially resource-rich, labor-scarce lands (Congo and Rhodesia in Africa; Colombia and Venezuela in Latin America; Indonesia and Malaysia in Asia) where, according to the law of supply and demand, wages should have risen, as they did in Australia, Canada, New Zealand, and the United States—white regions of "recent settlement."[14] The American South and Brazil went as far as using slavery to keep labor docile.

Divisions within the Third World widened over time due to a colonial inheritance—the presence or absence of manufacturing experience. The power of the manufacturing mind is illustrated by the Axis powers. Germany, Italy, and Japan all recovered after defeat in war on the basis of their memory—all physical infrastructure had been destroyed; only experience mattered.

On the eve of decolonization, manufacturing experience was greatest in Argentina, Brazil, Chile, China, Korea, Malaysia, Mexico, India, Indonesia, Taiwan, Thailand, and Turkey. Many of these countries had gained their manufacturing knowledge as a consequence of either Japan's preparations for war or inward emigration from Europe, China, and the United States. While not every country with prewar manufacturing experience succeeded (Argentina bombed), no country without it could create a diversity of advanced industries in the half-century after World War II.

Manufacturing experience implied the existence of entrepreneurs, managers, engineers, lawyers, accountants, an educated elite, a big student population, and a large working class in urban areas. These were the interest groups that typically took up the struggle for democracy. Students led the revolution for democracy in Korea in 1960 and 1987. Workers and students challenged Beijing's authority in Tiananmen Square in 1989 (the students wanting more political reform, the workers wanting less). Students "disappeared" in droves during Latin America's fight against tyranny in the 1970s. India, with one of the largest manufacturing elites, was extraordinary for democratizing as early as 1947. A big effort was soon launched to become self-sufficient in food. Certain industries were reserved for small- and medium-sized enterprise, with disastrous effects. China is the main exception, but even China developed activist grassroots politics. Rural countries may be democracies; the Ivory Coast was one for years. But if industry gets too small, if unemployment gets too large, and if upward mobility becomes blocked, democracy will be defeated (democracy in the Ivory Coast fell to tribal rivalries).

The manufacturing class has been weak in many Arab and African countries. In 1956, one estimate suggests there were only 143 local doctors and 41 engineers in Tunisia, a country with 4 million people. In Morocco, with 10 million people, there were 19 Muslim and 17 Moroccan Jewish doctors, and 15 Muslim and 15 Moroccan Jewish engineers. As more professionals were trained, more migrated for lack of good jobs, leading to a vicious circle of insufficient skills and hence insufficient investment in modern industry and services, and a weak lobby for political reform.[15] In the Arab world, only 4 countries out of 17 have multiparty electoral systems. In sub-Saharan Africa, the share is 29 out of 42.[16]

"Civilizing patterns" in Western countries typically went from political advance (the Magna Carta in England), to economic advance (the first Industrial Revolution), to the welfare state. The sequence has been entirely different in the Third World. Here, the pattern has typically gone from paternalism (the Latin American *hacienda*), to economic development, to democracy. But as income distribution widens between the richest and the poorest countries, democracy in the Third World takes on a new imperative. It must include elections at home as well as transparency in the foreign economic policies that constrain them. Which is more difficult to achieve—democracy at home, or democratization of the U.S. Treasury, World Bank, IMF, and World Trade Organization? This is an open question.

VIII Guns, Germs, and Steel

Jared Diamond examines early societies in terms of "guns, germs, and steel."[17] In the ancient world that he masterfully analyzes, nothing existed that was close to what is now essential for survival: formal, institutional, national systems of innovation. The most successful latecomers started out with prewar manufacturing experience and then added layer after layer of all kinds of skills—production, project execution, managerial, technological, bureaucratic, and political. Skills had to be systematically strengthened to kill the germs, make the steel, and ward off the guns of the great powers.

Both Arnold Toynbee and Edward Gibbon saw empires dying from within: from "suicide" in Toynbee's view and from "immoderation" in Gibbon's. The First American Empire paid dearly for ignorance and immoderation; it died from a lack of understanding of a people's war in Vietnam. Still, power was preserved by the United States after its fall. The Second American Empire is now in decline, possibly from immoderation but principally from a *lack of greatness*: it has made little contribution to economic development due to what may be described as a closed mind. Can its way of thinking be changed, or is it too late?

2 Where the Sun Never Sets, and Wages Never Rise

There exists no government by which so much is written and so little done, as the Government of India.

Karl Marx, *New York Daily Tribune,* 1853

I A Hidden Clue

Years after colonialism collapsed, it is still being complimented and justified for spreading civilization to the earth's uncouth corners. America's empires rest on a similar defense, which is why greatness should be measured by how much an empire civilizes, or encourages economic growth.[1] But do European and Japanese colonialists in fact deserve flattery? Aside from exporting ideas such as free trade and Asian co-prosperity, which shouldn't have required the use of force, did they teach the practical arts of innovating, engineering, and marketing? Were colonies given access to the assets that were necessary for them to outcompete their colonizers? Or were skills for the asking and never a nuisance to obtain, as the classical and neoclassical economists assumed? It is impossible to say whether the "uncouth" would have been better off colonized or left alone, but historians have uncovered much about colonialism's enduring drag on development. Japan, always independent, stands out as a success case compared to India, the jewel in England's crown.

Following the invention of DDT and a partial cure for malaria, Europeans could penetrate beyond the coastlines of their colonies, driving deep into the heart of darkness, as Joseph Conrad called it. Railroads were built. Technological innovations from the North were applied to mines and plantations. Techniques emerged that were superior to the primitive methods used by locals, such as Malaya's Chinese tin miners. Synthetics like rubber replaced more expensive natural materials, bankrupting rubber-producing countries like Liberia.

The rush was on. But the non-European and non-Japanese witnesses to all of this stayed backward or fell behind.

Starting with the first Industrial Revolution, the income gap under colonialism widened between rich and poor countries. Even the educated elite of the developing world fell behind, or were transformed from local rebels to law enforcers—the princes, the teachers, doctors, clerics, civil servants, and landowners, the merchants, mechanics, and moneylenders that comprised the middle class. Without a surge in domestic economic growth, foreign profits from mineral extraction and agriculture had no reason to remain behind and were repatriated back home. This was a death knell for learning, because investments in new plant and equipment are the reason behind acquiring technology. Unless technology is going to be used, it is pointless to acquire it.

The textile exports of India, a colony, and Japan, a free country, were about tied in 1899. Soon Japan pulled ahead on a wide front, including the manufacture of silk (invented in China). Was foreign domination what made the difference, or was India always behind (setting aside its Mughal Empire), busy learning the ABCs of British democracy?

These questions are too numerous to be answered in one short book, but two clues about the factors that are really important for development keep arising. They are hidden in a paragraph by an eminent historian, Edmund Silberner:

> For more than a century, when the British economy was on its way to maturity as the workshop of the world, its governments were not particularly liberal nor wedded ideologically to laissez-faire. Like the proverbial hedgehog of Aeschylus, the Hanoverian Governments [1688–1815] knew some big things, namely that security, trade, Empire and military power really mattered. In fruitful (if uneasy) partnership with bourgeois merchants and industrialists they poured millions into strategic objectives which we can see (with hindsight) formed preconditions for the market economy and night-watchman state of Victorian England, as well as the British world order which flourished under British hegemony from 1846 to 1914. By that time men of the pen, especially the pens of the political economy, had forgotten, and did not wish to be reminded, what the first industrial nation owed to men of the sword.[2]

II In the Red

Being short of money was one reason that empires repeatedly said "no" to funding development projects. Imperialism wasn't cheap. An empire's up-keep, especially maintaining law and order, was a huge fiscal burden: "The liquor tax was a significant source of revenue; and police, jails, and courts were among the major items of expenditure."[3] Spending on law and order was a high priority because of pervasive civil unrest throughout colonial history: Haiti's war of independence as early as 1804, the Sepoy Mutiny in India in 1857, and the Boxer Rebellion in China in 1899–1900 were the bloodiest and costliest uprisings of all. But lesser examples abound; the Ashanti War of 1873–74; the Zulu War of 1879; the 1919 nationalist uprising in Korea; protests in Rhodesia against settler land expropriations in the 1930s; Gandhi's civil disobedience movement in India; Nigeria's Satiru uprising in the north in 1906, its Abeokuta protests of 1917, its Abe women's tax riots in 1929, and a bloody coal miners strike in 1946; communist insurgency in China beginning in the 1920s, communist guerrilla movements in Malaya in the 1940s, and communist civil war in the Philippines and Vietnam in the 1950s; Kenya's Mau Mau uprising in 1954, not to mention ongoing peasant resistance in the form of foot-dragging, false compliance, crop neglect, and sabotage.[4]

Almost 30 percent of Europe's savings—a huge sum of money—became available for overseas investment by the time of World War I. But almost all of it went to white "regions of recent settlement"—Australia, the United States (north of the Mason-Dixon line), Canada, New Zealand, Rhodesia, and South Africa. Africa and Asia got $11 per capita compared with $131 per capita in European offshoots. The irrigation and expertise required to raise "native" crop yields remained at "entirely inadequate levels." Meanwhile, overseas industry, in the throes of a second revolution up north, attracted microscopic amounts of foreign money. The textile industry that began to develop along modern lines in China and India was financed by a local business elite.[5]

Besides a shortage of cash, there was an acute shortage of democracy, putting decision-making power in the hands of foreigners: "From the seventeenth century onward, the British, the Dutch and the French rightly conceived of themselves as having elaborated and integrated into their societies an understanding of political freedom, and yet during this very period they pursued and held vast empires where such freedoms were either absent or severely attenuated for the majority of the native inhabitants."[6] Not only were colonies not given much for investment, they were not given much leeway politically to fend for themselves.

In the run-of-the-mill colony, the Industrial Revolution that was transforming Europe and its offshoots was virtually unknown. Maybe modern law was established. Maybe Galileo was taught in the most elite schools. But overall, education was primitive. In 1950, adult *ill*iteracy was 3 to 4 percent in the United Kingdom, Belgium, and the United States, but 51 percent in Brazil, 62 percent in Malaya, and as high as 83 percent in India.[7] Still, close examination of Europe's nineteenth-century technology suggests that, at the time, primary education was not important for economic growth.[8] Even in Europe and the United States, formal education was not highly regarded. Skills were acquired on the job, but the problem was that in the colonies there were very few jobs.

European colonies suffered from a "color bar" that emaciated the class of professionals and entrepreneurs that was necessary for modernization. In employment, the color bar "was a major obstacle, since it limited the experience of talented people, and was a constraint on the development of administrative capacity."[9] It also worked in such a way that critical state support to local enterprising industrialists was never forthcoming. In 1970, Sir W. Arthur Lewis, a Nobel laureate in economics from St. Lucia, argued, "There were some positive results in the better colonies—schools, the introduction of scientific technologies, modernization of legal systems, strengthening of administrative structures, and so on." But, he continues, "for the most part colonialism was an additional obstacle to modernization, not merely because of the prevailing attitude of neglect, but because of the preference of the imperial powers (excluding Japan) for backing and ruling through the existing hierarchies—princely, land-owning or religious—at the expense of emerging liberals or radicals."[10] By colluding with traditional sources of power and repressing the liberals and radicals, the colonialists retarded the rise of an agenda for industrialization, agricultural modernization, and democracy.

Europeans were favored over locals not just in employment but also in business, education, and politics. Modern services, such as international shipping, fell entirely into European and American hands. Before 1850,

Indians ruled the Indian Ocean's waves. But Indian shipping, D. R. Headrick writes in *The Tentacles of Progress*, "was almost completely eclipsed after 1850 by ships owned by Europeans. . . . The problem was not simply one of economic efficiency. The world of shipping was always highly political, and if French, Italian or Japanese lines survived, it is because they had significant help from their respective governments. Potential Indian ship owners found their government consistently favoring their strongest competitors, the British lines."[11]

The railroads that transported the colonial world's mineral wealth and export crops to seagoing ports promised to spawn a new managerial and technological elite. Railroads themselves were the first industry to develop professional management: "the capital required to build a railroad was far more than that required to purchase a plantation, a textile mill, or even a fleet of ships. Therefore, a single entrepreneur, family or small group of associates was rarely able to own a railroad. Nor could the many stockholders or their representatives manage it. The administrative tasks were too numerous, too varied, and too complex. They required special skills and training which could only be commanded by a full-time salaried manager."[12]

With a rail system more extensive than that of any other colony, India derived minimal technological capabilities from its railroads. According to Headrick, "The successful manufacture of locomotives in India and the considerable export of used locomotives from India to countries in Africa, Southeast Asia and the Mid East are evidence that India had a potential comparative advantage in this industry. Yet the railway workshops built only 4 percent of the locomotives used in British India. Another 14,420 locomotives—almost 80 percent—were imported from Britain. This was not the result of market forces, but of policy decisions."[13] As late as the 1920s, "the mechanical engineers on the Indian railroads were all Europeans; Indians were not welcome into the profession."[14]

In both Kuwait and Bahrain in the 1930s, M. Wilkins writes in *The Maturing of Multinational Enterprise*, "Americans ran their oil operations through 'British' companies: The Bahrein Petroleum Company employed in large part a British staff; the Kuwait Oil Company, half-owned by British capital, likewise had a preponderance of British managers." Americans owned about one-fourth of the Iraq Petroleum Company in the 1930s, and "American drillers worked at the Kirkuk field in the North. The pipeline from Kirkuk to Tripoli and Haifa was constructed by American engineers using American materials. Iraq Petroleum's operating management was primarily British." In Mexico, a commission to smooth labor relations in the oil industry observed that the overwhelming majority of oil drillers in Mexico were foreigners and that "it is advisable to oblige the oil companies [the major form of foreign direct investment in the 1930s] to utilize the services of Mexican technicians."[15] Mexico nationalized its oil industry in 1938, which led to a boycott by the major international oil companies that kept Mexico's oil industry out of commission *until the 1970s*.

Even when the word "color" was absent from policy, its discriminatory meaning was clear. In the case of Malaya's rubber industry, M. Rudner argues, "So far as British planting circles were concerned, the smallholders' capacity to produce rubber at prices below the profitability threshold of estates instilled fear that the Malayan rubber industry would eventually 'go native.' This fear inspired leading British planters to utilize their access to centres of colonial political authority to obtain policies aimed at protecting the capital values of the estate sector. The international rubber restriction schemes, originally intended to maintain export prices, accordingly came to be applied in colonial Malaya as a calculated device for undermining the long-run competitive position of peasant smallholdings."[16]

As another example of discriminatory policy, two-thirds of a government experimental tea garden in India was transferred rent-free to a British monopolist in 1836. Thereafter, D. Banerjee explains, "the British planters kept on increasing their share in the industry under the direct and unrelenting patronage of the colonial government." While the peasants paid heavy land taxes, the Europeans paid none.[17]

Any kind of "bar," blockage, ban, or barrier impedes the flow of knowledge. But the colonial color bar was especially pernicious because it penalized the most capable of the nonwhite population. Even when the native elites of colonies were co-opted into high positions in the local colonial administration, as they were by the Raj, their role was divisive. Britain's "divide and rule" policies included pitting one part of the local ruling elite against another, thereby weakening the emergence of a dynamic, unified middle class.

Manufacturing experience in Japan's colonies, historically related to war, was acquired more easily than in Europe's colonies. During World War I, European exports to Asia were blocked. Demand rose for Japanese products, but capacity was too small to meet demand. Japan looked to its colonies for help, relaxing a 1911 law that forbade industries in Korea to compete against industries in Japan. Japanese big business invested in Korean textiles and cement. Modernization was under way and, unlike Britain, Japan promoted colonial manufacturing.

III Nothing Doing

Making matters worse for Europe's colonies, the rich were lightly taxed and the poor were fed too little to be milked. Private wealth went hand in hand with public destitution. The result was an attitude of neglect, with government doing as little as decency allowed. Physical infrastructure was built by the military or by unscrupulous private contractors, much like those who operate today in Afghanistan or Iraq.

Egyptian industry "could only surmount the obstacles it faced with a considerable degree of official support, which in the period up to 1914 *was almost entirely lacking*" (emphasis added)."[18] This was in spite of the manufacturing experience Egypt had acquired under Muhammed Ali in the 1830s, a precocious experiment that included factories, arsenals, and schools, all put out of business by immaturity, militarism, and Britain's malicious use of taxes and duties.

Agriculture, supposedly the colonies' comparative advantage, received little help either. According to Nobel laureate W. A. Lewis, "to exploit the farmers a government would first have to make them productive, which meant introducing cash crops and opening up land with roads or irrigation. This colonial governments conspicuously failed to do."[19]

Force and neglect created a Molotov cocktail, as many new colonial histories suggest. Peasant unrest flared when farmers were forced by administrative fiat to plant more cash crops for exporting and fewer food crops for eating, leading to export booms but threats of famine. As T. J. Bassett states, in the case of cotton, "output levels were often correlated with levels of coercion. When forced cultivation ebbed, output levels declined."[20] The Ivory Coast was targeted as a source of cotton for the French textile industry, which wanted a reliable substitute for American cotton. But African growers could get a higher price for their cotton locally because of demand from prosperous local artisans, whose exports to the Sahara benefited from the exceptional quality of cotton locally grown. To insure a supply of cotton for export, the French colonial administration resorted to force. Force also characterized cotton growing in Mali (the French Soudan) and Mozambique (under Portuguese rule). Brazil, like the U.S. South, depended on slavery.

When the railroad in the Ivory Coast reached the city of Bouaké in 1912, Bassett writes, "cotton and other crops were swiftly imposed on the peoples of the savanna." District guards forced peasants to double the size of their rice fields and to plant 500 hectares of cotton. Peasants were "advised" to reserve two-thirds of their fields for cotton plants. The French governor of the region believed in "scientific" methods, meaning monocropping cotton in rows, which made it easier for district guards to delimit cotton fields and to supervise their cultivation. The disobedient were flogged. A "commander's field" was established to exploit unpaid African labor. If peasants underperformed on these fields, "guards often singled out lineage heads of production units, forced them to lie on the ground, and whipped them. Some were forced to carry heavy rocks on their heads throughout the village."[21] Burdening Africans still further, chiefs of residential areas had to give colonial administrators free sacks of rice, maize, millet, and peanuts. In the absence of any improvement in farming methods, compulsory cropping meant an immediate reduction in resources available for food intake.[22] Peasants were without a voice, despite talk of democracy. Village chiefs were given bonuses, credit, and commissions by both the French and British as rewards for collecting more tribute.

With little money to spend, colonial governments stooped even lower. In colonies with rich raw materials and more demand for labor than what was available (such as Malaya, Kenya, Rhodesia, Zambia, and South Africa), dirty deeds were done to get more hands. To force locals into paid employment, at lower-than-market rates, households were taxed or their land was appropriated. Taxing Africans and taking away their land, as was done in Congo—the worst case—Rhodesia, South Africa, and Kenya, forced men to work for "a bachelor wage," which was calculated down to the calorie by the London School of Tropical Hygiene. They labored at long distances, which forced women to farm alone at home. This led to low productivity, divided families, prostitution, penury, and disease.[23] Years later, when the AIDS epidemic erupted in South and Central Africa, colonial policies from the 1930s that had divided households made the epidemic easier to spread. Whereas labor-scarce white regions of recent settlement like Australia and

New Zealand developed high-wage economies, their nonwhite cohorts became low-wage economies through force and lack of training.

When colonial administrations coughed up cash for irrigation and railroads, the burden of indebtedness was catastrophic. According to one Iraqi, interviewed in 1909: "It is the same old story. The drama of Egypt [which Britain annexed in 1882] shall be reenacted in Iraq [as indeed happened]. First comes the irrigation scheme. Then, all of a sudden, it will be discovered it will be no good to make the soil productive unless there are the means of exporting. . . . To achieve this purpose railways must be established. . . . Then there is the question of money. The foreign promoter obtains permission to raise a loan in England. The loan is raised, irrigation and railway schemes are completed. New schemes crop up and the loan is never repaid. Military intervention becomes imperative; India, with its standing colonial army, is near, and occupation follows. Iraq becomes Egypt!"[24]

IV Entrepreneurship

When the force of the market, not the machete, assumed control, the quality of foreign technology transfer improved. But it was still problematic.

In the 1880s several Anglo-Brazilian sugar factories were promoted by railroad contractors and were universally a flop: "Contemporary opinion was unanimous in regarding the direction of these companies as deplorable," R. Graham writes, although the financial success of some *Brazilian* sugar factories suggested that it was possible to run them successfully.[25] Even the big trading companies, which preceded the multinationals, were not especially effective in their technology transfer. In China, two British silk mills were brought into being by prominent British trading companies, Jardine, Matheson & Co. and Kungping Co., but they quickly went out of business because of poor management.[26] On the other hand, in an Indonesian town, a successful mechanized "Javanese sugar" factory "became owned by a small landlord and political leader and operated by a man who was for a short time a technician in a Dutch sugar mill, with a Chinese accountant to keep the books."[27]

Sometimes the effectiveness of the foreign technicians was constrained by culture and social disparities. In the case of the Ottoman Empire in the 1850s, "Christian Europeans simply were not the most effective role models and were unpersuasive as opinion leaders, even in those instances when they knew the language. Their advice often was ignored. In many cases, the hired technicians believed their job was to run the equipment and not necessarily to teach new skills. The enormous wage differentials between foreign and Ottoman workers that were typical contributed to poor relations between the two groups."[28]

Ironically, many foreign firms did not excel in entrepreneurialism. They followed rather than led local firms in opening new industries. When foreign firms finally replaced foreign individuals as technology providers, they were more likely to enter a foreign market to enjoy an ongoing process rather than to be a first mover and act as a catalyst for industrial expansion. For example, direct British investment in Brazil followed the lead of Brazilian pioneers,[29] and in the case of Mexican railways, "local companies constructed a total of 226 kilometers of track before North American capital arrived to construct the country's two major arteries."[30] Ultimately, American and European multinationals invested heavily in the manufacturing industries of Latin America, particularly in consumer goods, but when they did so in large numbers, beginning in the 1910s or 1920s, many modern industries had already been founded.[31] Most Latin American cigarette firms were established in the early years of the twentieth century and some in the 1890s. They grew rapidly in Argentina, Brazil, Chile, and Mexico. In these markets, the largest in the region, British-American Tobacco Ltd. gained a beachhead either just before or after the First World War, frequently by acquiring a local firm.[32] The founders of Argentina's meatpacking industry included one British firm as well as two local firms; two of the three were taken over in 1907 by American packers.[33] The Corning Glassworks and the Pittsburgh Glass Company bought controlling interest in Argentina's financially strapped Cristalerías Rigolleau company in 1942, thereby acquiring "an old and prestigious firm that already enjoyed a commanding position in its field and established connections with both suppliers and buyers."[34]

In China, except for a couple of unsuccessful attempts, no textile mill owned by a Westerner was established until 1914, whereas modern Chinese mills began appearing in the 1890s. Japanese investments in China's cotton mills were takeovers; the Chinese themselves were the trailblazers.[35] Foreign firms invested in Chinese industries other than textiles, but such firms initially tended to be very small, with no notable names of multinational manufacturers among them. Foreign investors were not the first movers in Japan, either; they did not enter the country until the period from 1896 to World War I, "when the Japanese had already demonstrated their general progressive drive and their specific industrial aptitudes."[36]

In India, foreign individuals were responsible for starting the jute industry, a major nineteenth-century exporter, and for initiating railroad construction. But Indians took the lead in creating the cotton textile, power generation, shipping, construction, sugar, iron and steel, engineering, agricultural implements, and later chemical, automobile, and aircraft industries. Initially London would not allow India to develop its own steel industry, for fear that it would displace British steel exports to India. When such exports were challenged by German steel, a domestic steel industry became acceptable. The British "must have thought that the abolition of the irksome prospecting laws would induce English entrepreneurs to set up steel plants in India. However, only one Englishman made a feeble attempt to enter the field," and India's first steel mill, noted earlier, was built by one of the biggest entrepreneurial Indian families today, the Tatas.[37]

In Turkey, the "foreigners" who often established modern production facilities were actually émigrés who had lived in the Ottoman Empire for generations. For example, the largest textile factory built in Izmir before 1912–13 was owned by a descendant of old French and English commercial families active in the Izmir region since the late eighteenth and early nineteenth centuries.[38] Ironically, truly foreign investment in Turkey began only after native non-Muslims were driven out of the country following World War I by nationalists (the Young Turks) who hoped to create a larger economic role for native Muslim capitalists. Instead, foreign investors filled the breach and eventually accounted for 63 percent of manufacturing output.[39]

In theory, foreign firms are desirable because they provide "spillovers" and a positive role model. As one historian wrote in 1930, "One cannot go into the Chinese-owned [textile] mills in China without realizing the influence of the Japanese-owned mills."[40] Nevertheless, foreign investors did not necessarily take the lead, nor were foreign role models above crushing domestic competition. In China's cigarette industry, British American Tobacco (BAT), a giant multinational, and Nanyang, a local firm, competed head-on in the 1910s for China's growing market. Chien Chao-nan, the owner of Nanyang, put a deposit on a warehouse in the foreign concession area of Shanghai to begin production. (Nanyang had accumulated experience producing cigarettes in Hong Kong using Japanese technology.) According to historian S. Cochran, "The very next day a BAT comprador tried to buy the building," which started a vehement argument that ended only when one of BAT's own compradors (a Cantonese like Chien) "defended Nanyang's position and urged BAT's management not to force Chien to surrender his rights to the building." Chien installed 119 American cigarette-making machines and later bought the site.[41] In another case, in the 1890s entrepreneurs who attempted to manufacture textiles in the Ottoman Empire for local consumption (in Egypt) were brought to bankruptcy by the pressure of lobbyists for Manchester textile interests. The British ambassador first attempted to block the mill's construction with administrative delays, but then, to insure his own reappointment against threats from English textile manufacturers, acted more vigorously in getting the local government to impose high production taxes on the mill. Construction was halted.[42]

In industries experiencing fast technological change (such as textiles), an engineering orientation on the part of management was essential to keep abreast of new developments. Yet technological expertise was not necessarily a characteristic of foreign investors. Japan's first major steel works received technical assistance from Germany in 1897, but "the German engineers did not work as hard as the Yawata Works had expected. They lacked the basic knowledge and abilities to lead Japanese engineers and foremen." This was in spite of the fact that the chief engineer, earned a very high salary—twice as much as that of the prime minister of Japan! Yawata reached the conclusion that "the German engineers who came to the Far East were hardly first rate."[43] In Mexico, financing was provided by "a relatively small clique of [European] merchant-financiers who, because of their backgrounds in commerce and money-lending, were more adept at rigging the market and manipulating government policy than at streamlining production methods or innovating new processes or techniques."[44] Foreign firms accounted for roughly 20 percent of the output in India's textile industry, but they were hardly exemplary models. Few directors either in European-owned mills or Indian-owned mills had a technical background; commercial backgrounds in both cases were the norm.

Just as teaching in technology transfers was far from ideal, learning was also imperfect due to insufficient local investments to absorb foreign skills. In 1890, about 60 percent of all technical personnel in the middle management of Bombay textile mills was European, and as late as the 1920s, roughly one-third of all such managers remained foreign. Apparently, Indians had not acquired enough expertise to dispense with the services of foreign advisers. Although the Mexican textile industry had started in the 1830s, in the 1890s "foreign visitors commented that plants were managed by an Englishman with sound Lancashire experience or by men trained in the Manchester district of England. In 1896 a new plant in Torreón brought in forty skilled workers from France."[45] One of Brazil's largest cotton mills, America Fabril, was started by two merchants and an industrialist in 1878. But as late as 1921 its managing director was a Yorkshireman and more than 40 English foremen were engaged in various departments.[46] In contrast, between 1914 and 1922, China witnessed an increase in its spindles and looms of over 300 percent, and most of the mills in this period were able to save money and hire Chinese engineers rather than foreign technicians.[47] Similarly, in 1900 the British-owned Rio Flour Mills in Brazil reported that through a training program many Brazilians had learned the trade, so that "all our millers, engineers, and other skilled workmen, with the exception of less than half a dozen, and all our ordinary workmen to the number of about 250, are natives of, or permanently settled in the country."[48] A similar pattern evolved at the Osaka Spinning Company, which began to produce yarn in 1883: "as always, an English engineer came to direct the installation of the spinning machines. A foreign engineer working at the mint in Osaka came to help with the installation of the steam engines. But a Japanese engineer also joined in, so the installation did not completely depend on foreign engineers. The age of complete dependence on foreigners was passing"[49]—at least in Japan, the paramount country that industrialized independent of colonial rule.

V Imperial Gardens

Scientific farming arrived in the colonial world with the plantation. Most public investments in agronomy were designed to help large, professionally managed estates to increase their yields, reduce disease, and diversify crops.

Botanical gardens appeared in the nineteenth century in order to acclimatize new plants—a Dutch garden in Java, a British one in Ceylon, and another British one in India for the tea industry. The first state universities in the United States were based on agricultural extension services starting in the 1840s. The great Kew Gardens outside London acted as a central distributing center. It cultivated a hardy rubber plant and sent millions of seeds to British tropical colonies ranging from Borneo to Burma and the West Indies. Toward the end of the nineteenth century, the work of importing new cultures began to give way to research, and the botanical stations ceased to be only acclimatizing centers and became instead great scientific laboratories that employed chemists, entomologists, mycologists, botanists, veterinary surgeons, and agricultural engineers. As one historian wrote, "Some of the greatest successes were obtained by working upon indigenous plants, picking out the best strains, crossing them, and breeding new plants along Mendelian lines."[50]

In Japan, R. H. Myers and Y. Saburo note, "farmers gradually began to acquire a new farming technology with new capital such as high-yield, disease-resistant rice seeds, fertilizers, farm implements, and means for eradicating pests." Because Japan's colonies, Taiwan and Korea, also specialized in rice and were meant to serve as Japan's rice bowl, it was prudent to transfer technological knowledge to them, and relatively easy to do so in light of their high educational attainments. By 1898, the first agricultural experimentation station was established outside Taipei. By 1910, it had selected the 300 best rice varieties for planting out of 1,679 that it had discovered on the island.[51]

In 1890, experimental farms were a regular feature of the landscape even in Bihar, one of India's poorest regions. The impact of irrigation, fertilizer, ploughs, harrowing, and weeding were studied with respect to sugar, wheat, and other food crops. Unfortunately, the communication of such information was above the peasant's head, and experimental farming "had almost no impact on the surrounding areas." There was some success in spreading the use of varieties that peasants had seen growing well with their own eyes. But in the 1920s, one newspaper observed "very small holders who work on borrowed capital and who, even if they had the will, have not the means to carry out suggested improvements."[52] To achieve scientific improvements in peasant production, the state had to abandon laissez-faire: "In addition to education (some primary schools already had 'gardens' for experimentation, with schoolchildren expected to teach best techniques to their parents), the small holder who is to be induced to grow better or more produce needs Government assistance at every turn to provide credit, seed, instruction and help in marketing."[53] To induce "natives" in Uganda to grow coffee, for example, the British government bought their entire annual coffee crop. Dishonest traders were banned from dealing in groundnuts in Nigeria, where the government set up "fermentaries" for the cocoa bean. In the West Indies, the government established a ginnery for cotton and factories for crushing sugar.

Still, it is questionable how deep technical assistance to the peasantry went. "Government assistance at every turn" did not materialize. The poorest farmers, who concentrated on producing foodstuffs, got virtually no help. On the other hand, the peasants who were given better seeds didn't necessarily increase their own know-how about how to select seeds with the highest yield. They could use the seeds but not generate them, and they could plant the seeds but not know the principles of optimum planting.

The absence of a local elite of farming experts seriously handicapped technology transfer. Even if the wisdom now is that primary schooling was unnecessary for catching up in the nineteenth century, agricultural experts were a must. Here the numbers are disgraceful: "The first technical college in the Gold Coast [Ghana] opened in 1951, six years before independence. South of the Sahara, only one college [in South Africa] was open to Africans before World War II. In Portuguese Angola and Mozambique, the most backward of the colonies, 86 Africans were attending secondary level technical schools in the mid-1950s, and two had become engineers by 1961." Frustrating the spread of scientific farming everywhere was a shortage of indigenous agronomists: "At Independence, British colonies in tropical Africa had only 150 graduates in agronomy, and the French colonies had only 4."[54]

In fact, a small middle class did emerge out of the boom in tropical exports from 1899 to 1913. It included traders, moneylenders, tax collectors, shopkeepers, municipal officials, builders, harbor masters, teachers, and others among the upwardly mobile population. They fueled the nationalist movements that began to seethe around the issue of independence. But these elites were not professional, and generally lacked the engineering and business know-how that was necessary to put agriculture and manufacturing on a modern footing. The color bar continued to shut out the colonial world's indigenous talent from owning or managing professional firms and plantations, or participating in Western culture.

The British regarded agriculture as the comparative advantage of its colonies; Britain itself would produce the higher value-added manufactures. Although peasant farming had its moments of fair weather, over time, as output increased and synthetic substitutes arose, commodity prices fell and agriculture was less a source of savings for industry than a sinkhole for low productivity and back-bending work.

Still, big farming underwent a major change in the nineteenth century, becoming more productive with government help. The model of laissez-faire, which had originated in agriculture, was displaced by the model of government support to agro-industry. This paragon later became the Green Revolution. Ultimately, the government's model of support to agriculture would be transferred to industry proper, heralding the rise of state-driven industrialization.

VI Chasing after the Clue

There are few incidents in colonial history related to the formation of capitalist markets. Farmers in central Africa had to be dragged kicking and screaming into the labor market, but only because they were forced into it at below market prices. Markets are upheld as the lost ark of economic development, but there isn't much evidence that they were fiercely difficult to form.

Control over the use of force, governance, administrative power, authority, the color bar, and entrenched rule provide one clue to economic development. Control is what colonialism is all about and is what led to Britain's rise. The Hanoverian kings had it, weighed it, used it, and won a huge prize. Power over policies and decision making runs through the Third World's struggle for technological knowledge. The less the Third World has of it, the less it can grow. The textile industries of China and India, feathers in the cap of latecomers, did well because they could circumvent imperial do-nothingness with their own money. The regions of recent settlement raced ahead because they were on the same wavelength socially and politically as their imperialist sisters. Argentina, Brazil, Chile, and Mexico could gain manufacturing experience because they were no longer colonized, and they could attract foreign immigrants more or less on their own terms. Japan outpaced India because it controlled its own fate. It was perilously behind the great powers after Perry's opening in 1868, so it dropped out, deliberately industrialized under a unified state (unlike India's divided Maharajas), and then roared back into world markets.

Hanoverian Britain was not only strong but also smart. As Silberner notes, "the Hanoverian Governments knew some big things" about development.[55] Knowledge is one clue to how countries grow. Europe became what it was because of its industrial revolutions. Its colonies learned, but they learned small things, not big things. Even Japan's colonies were industrialized only in preparation for war, when Japan's enemies also industrialized their colonies in defense. Over the long haul of prewar imperialism, only 12 out of over 100 developing countries gained enough know-how to be described as experienced manufacturers. This says little for the spread of civilization and a lot for the control of knowledge!

The First American Empire fits right into this argument. After World War II, the developing world grew at unprecedented rates because the First American Empire gave it more leeway to control its own fate than at any time in the past. Under the strongest empire in creation, a Third World "lite" racked its brains for ideas on how to industrialize—and found them.

3 Trading Earth for Heaven

Jean Monnet, the apostle of European economic integration, said one day while walking with my wife and me, "Bernstein [chief U.S. economist and Keynes's counterpart at Bretton Woods], who's going to run the International Monetary Fund?" I said, "Mr. Gutt is going to be the first managing director." He said, "I don't mean that, Eddy. I mean who, at the Treasury, is going to run the International Monetary Fund?"

Edward Bernstein, *A Levite among the Priests*

I A Refreshing Change

The First American Empire came out of World War II as an unorthodox thinker and cold warrior. This was one of the many contradictions of the age: the United States became anticommunist to a maniacal degree, but within the bounds of capitalism, it became amenable to heterodox ideas. Even its clash with communism produced heterodox policies to win the hearts and minds of the world's poor people, the "Third World." At first, the United States took potshots at the Third World's development plans. Then it came to terms with a revisionist definition of laissez-faire: "do it your way."

Big science, research and development, higher education, the GI Bill, tuition-free state colleges, and TV quiz shows all respected the brain and encouraged experimentation. An anti-intellectual theme in American culture became an intellectual countertheme, which approved of trying out new ideas. The International Monetary Fund (IMF) and World Bank, formed at Bretton Woods in 1944, and the United Nations, founded in San Francisco in 1945, were institutions in tune with the times. The formation of both was novel in and of itself. They bowed to the biggest power and, for a brief spell, their policies were agile.

The Third World benefited from all these currents and crosscurrents. If it stayed within the capitalist camp, it could deviate from the free-market norm, shift around and sort out its own policies, exploiting insights about itself. It was freer than ever before in recent history, and its growth became faster.

The brain trust of Franklin Roosevelt and the Harvard brain trust of John Kennedy comprised academics who legitimized heterodoxy. Roosevelt called the financial and economic elites who had nearly torpedoed his New Deal the "Royalists," and because of this domestic history their stabs at the Third World's "statist" policies carried less weight than they might otherwise have done. A leading New Dealer and Columbia professor, Rexford G. Tugwell, experimented with development planning in Puerto Rico. Kennedy appointed Harvard iconoclast John Kenneth Galbraith as ambassador to India. Even Republican administrations tolerated some deviation abroad. President Eisenhower's main adviser, his brother Milton, had worked for FDR and then became president of Johns Hopkins University. As educator, he thought of Latin America in terms of not free markets but free tractors. President Richard Nixon summed up U.S. policy on the Third World, aside from Vietnam, very nicely: "People don't give a damn."

The First American Empire's deliberate oversight of the letter of trade law was instrumental in Third World growth. Washington let "reciprocity" slip. Developing countries were allowed more favorable trading terms than developed countries, and could industrialize behind tariff walls. This approach was the very opposite of the strait-laced trade policies that the Second American Empire would adopt, in which developed and developing countries would face identical rules. As Anatole France described the majesty of French law in the nineteenth century, a rich man and a poor man were punished equally for sleeping under a bridge.

Real freedom to decide on policies was crucial for the commencement of economic growth. But how did it all hang together, and could it ever be repeated?

II Winds of Change

American voices against colonialism grew louder and more diverse over time. According to A. Philip Randolph, a militant black organizer of the

Brotherhood of Sleeping Car Porters, World War II was "not a war for freedom. It was a war to continue 'white supremacy' and the . . . exploitation of people of color."[1] The executive secretary of the National Association for the Advancement of Colored People, Walter White, urged Roosevelt to pressure Britain to grant India independence as early as 1942 (it finally won independence in 1947). White also called for an end to colonial empires in Southeast Asia once Japan had been defeated, drew attention to the racism of white troops in China, and condemned Australia for its "whites only" immigration policy (black American GIs were harassed when they tried to land there). If, White warned, the war should end "with the continuing white lordship over brown, yellow and black peoples of the world," there would "inevitably be another war."[2]

The fight against racism in the United States itself, which led to the Supreme Court's *Brown v. Board of Education* decision in 1954 and passage of the Civil Rights Act in 1964, coincided with the struggle of nonwhite races for independence in the developing world. J. Goldstein and R. O. Keohane argue, "This is no mere coincidence. Third World intellectuals and politicians who were campaigning for decolonization were fully aware of these developments, and some of them were in direct contact with Western intellectuals and politicians (white and non-white) who were campaigning for racial equality within Western democracies."[3] Northern cities began to bow to black voters, and trade unions with a large black membership, such as the United Automobile Workers, began to support liberation. Soon decolonization became a major demand of American intellectuals, pulling in vocal supporters like Eleanor Roosevelt.

Disbelief or outright hostility in developing countries to the gospel of free trade was an integral part of the movement for independence. At a conference in Chapultepec, Mexico, in 1945, the United States preached the virtues of free trade to a "skeptical" Latin American audience. Yet Latin America—relatively rich and self-defined as part of the "West"—was probably closer to favoring free trade than even Asia, Africa, or the Middle East.[4] There, free trade, based on comparative advantage, was considered a deceit of the Devil. If poor countries already had raw materials and cheap labor, and if they continued to specialize in the export of raw materials and those manufactures embodying cheap labor, then they would never move ahead. Such primitive specialization didn't generate new skills, nor did it generate enough income to invest in skills because production was typically in the hands of foreigners. For the disadvantaged, specialization and comparative advantage were suffocating traps.

Soon even the Royalists began to soften. Decolonization was one of the great movements of the twentieth century, as scores of countries got self-government. England's last colonial prime minister, Harold Macmillan, described the movement as the "winds of change." Besides shaking up old political alliances and overturning old economic relations, decolonization won Washington's wholehearted yet cynical approval: the possibility for economic gain arose as Europe lost its monopolistic grip over its colonies, since American companies could then rush in to fill the breach.

American commitment to liberation was confirmed when France and England (and then Israel) invaded Egypt in 1956 to keep control of the Suez Canal. The United States, under the Eisenhower administration, sided with Egypt. Washington gave unflinching support to decolonization, except in Vietnam.

Decolonization brought to the fore developing countries on different continents that had different resources, population sizes and densities, geographies, histories, cultures, governments, and economies. The formulation of American foreign economic policy in the face of such heterogeneity was a nightmare. The United States had two realistic choices. It could impose free markets on all countries, a road that the Second American Empire took. This road was opposed by most developing countries and would have taken enormous effort to implement. It was also unlikely to generate rapid industrial growth without institutional reform that would have to vary from country to country. The second option was to let developing countries each do their own thing within capitalist bounds, with those bounds becoming tighter and tighter as the World Bank and IMF dirtied their hands.[5] The United States fell into following the second path.

III The Fight for Flexibility

Starting in the 1930s, the United States began to champion a policy of "trade, not aid" as the means to advance global economic growth. Aid was hopeless as a policy tool because it was nitpicked by Congress. Trade was preferable under the security-minded First American Empire, if only because it exhibited the same virtues that it had shown under British *"free trade imperialism."*[6] Open borders exposed a foreign country to close scrutiny, making transparent its economic policies, political factions, and military preparedness. Free trade made countries dependent on export markets, and the domestic market of the United States was the world's largest, giving Washington the greatest number of bargaining chips. In theory, free trade also offered developing countries an opportunity to grow, thus keeping them within the capitalist fold.

The guiding principle of America's trade policy was *reciprocity*: I open my markets and you open yours, in bilateral arrangements. In 1934, Congress passed a Reciprocal Trade Agreements Act that heralded the end of American isolationism and the beginning of an abiding devotion to free trade by *coercion*: instead of closing U.S. markets in retaliation for protectionism overseas, foreign countries were coerced to open their markets to U.S. goods—compulsory free trade.

The most ardent advocate of reciprocal free trade was Cordell Hull, a congressman from Tennessee who in 1933 was chosen by President Roosevelt to be secretary of state. Hull testified to the Senate Finance Committee that "unhampered trade dovetailed with peace; high tariffs, trade barriers, and unfair economic competition, with war."[7] The last year of Hull's tenure in office, 1944, coincided with the Bretton Woods international monetary conference. The United States was the largest financial donor to "the Bank" (as the World Bank is called), and thus enjoyed the power to appoint its president, who, in a top-down organization, held nearly absolute say over Bank policy. The same was true of the Inter-American Development Bank, which serviced Latin American borrowers. The United States was also a powerful director in the IMF, and typically appointed the second-in-command. Hull's ideas, therefore, slowly began to filter down to every continent as the Bretton Woods institutions lent to capital-starved developing countries, with the conditionality of free trade attached to their loans.

According to Dean Acheson, Harry Truman's secretary of state, "With almost fanatical single mindedness, he [Hull] devoted himself to getting legislative authority, and then acting upon it, to negotiate 'mutually beneficial reciprocal trade agreements' to reduce tariffs."[8] John Maynard Keynes referred to "the lunatic proposals of Mr. Hull."[9] Keynes believed that in times of depression and world strife, haggling over tariffs might inflame hostilities, whereas leaving tariffs in place might lead to peace. Contrary to popular belief, protection might *increase* trade, not decrease it. Industrialization needed raw materials, manufactured parts, components, and machinery. Some of these inputs would be purchased locally, others would be imported. If an industrializing country grew faster than under free trade by virtue of tariffs, it might import more of these inputs, not less. Trade would boom.

But free trade was the ideology of the First American Empire no less than that of the Second—or, for that matter, the British Empire before it. All these imperialists were children of the Enlightenment and knew one "big thing"—that free trade would benefit their own industries because they could outcompete anyone else's. How, then, could the First American Empire's approach to trade in the developing world be described as "flexible"? How could it be said that developing countries were free to choose their own industrialization policies, including trade policies, when the world's most powerful nation loved to make those choices for them?

IV A Piercing Glance

Slowly, foreign aid, soft loans, and technology transfer became sources of information about the Third World. U.S. understanding was strongest in the case of Latin America, due to long historical surveillance and the strength of multinational firms. It was weakest in Asia, whose languages were a nightmare to learn, whose foreign firms were few in number, and whose states were nationalistic.

It was not unusual for the World Bank to send its staff to participate *side by side* with the technocrats of a developing country, such as the Philippines, to help with economic planning. The American-driven Alliance for Progress was supposed to review each Latin American country's development plan. Following exchange rate difficulties in Thailand, the World Bank and IMF sent a "review team" in 1953 that began liberalizing Thailand's foreign trade. Finance ministers in countries ranging from Argentina to Egypt acquired their expertise by apprenticing at the IMF. With the bloody overthrow of the Sukarno regime in Indonesia in 1965 to 1967 and the assumption of power by a pro-Western military dictator, General Suharto, American-trained technocrats, called the Berkeley mafia, became responsible for Indonesia's economic opening to the West. After the bloody overthrow of Allende in Chile, a University of Chicago mafia became close consultants of the Pinochet dictatorship.

In South Korea, the U.S. embassy was located next door to Korea's Economic Planning Board, with an underground tunnel connecting the two. American economists reminisce of warm relations between the two countries, but Korea's superdevelopmental president, Park Chung Hee, wrote in his diaries of playing cat and mouse. In the late 1960s, the United States opposed Korea's investment in a shipyard on the grounds that it was too big (which it was). The shipyard is now the largest and possibly most efficient in the world, having diversified into steel structures, overhead cranes, and offshore platforms to absorb capacity. Ship designs were procured by Korea's ambassador to the United Kingdom, who drove around Scotland buying the designs of bankrupted Scottish shipbuilders. The United States also opposed Korea's investment in a steel mill on the grounds that it would create global excess capacity (meaning competition for U.S. steel corporations), and the World Bank turned down a loan for the project. The steel mill, now fourth largest in the world and possibly the most efficient, financed itself from Japanese war reparations. The United States opposed India's expulsion of IBM, which probably hurt India's computer industry but helped its software services (one of India's earliest software firms got its experience from servicing the computers IBM left behind). The United States harassed the Brazilian computer industry, which also banished IBM, but in any event Brazil specialized in the wrong type of computer.

Washington was on top of all this, and much more, observing Third World deviations from free trade and the rise of a new model of development. The flexibility of the First American Empire emerged fortuitously, not by design. The wisdom of the age finally let go.

V Tragic Stupidity

The developing world could grow rapidly under the First American Empire because Washington chose *not* to implement the principle of reciprocity, hoping that "redistributive trade" would win support for capitalism among the poor and sustain an attitude of indifference among the rich. The trade battles of the time were between the United States and Europe, not the United States and the developing world, but even trade negotiations with Europe were soft. With major exceptions, the United States opened its markets to the exports of developing countries but allowed developing countries to keep their markets protected from the exports of the United States. For an average commodity bundle, American tariffs plummeted, while those of its trading partners remained much higher. The average Third World American tariff on dutiable items declined from an all-time peak of nearly 60 percent in 1932, during the darkest days of the Depression, to only 12 percent in 1960, and then 3.5 percent in the 1990s.[10]

According to a former chairman of the U.S. International Trade Commission, Alfred E. Eckes, "During the Cold War years the United States treated trade policy as an instrument of foreign policy for fulfilling hegemonic responsibilities, not as an end in itself."[11] Time after time, U.S. diplomats and negotiators promoted one-sided trade liberalization in order to advance foreign-policy objectives—stability and prosperity in Japan and Western Europe, economic opportunities for developing nations. U.S. leaders stripped away tariff barriers but "allowed emerging competitors to waive parallel obligations and to maintain restrictive trade barriers, sheltering their national markets and corporate champions from U.S. competition."

This emphasis on opening the huge American market in order to help allies and promote reconstruction had emerged during World War II. Planners contemplated drastic and disproportionate cuts in U.S. tariffs to *stimulate imports*. A statute requiring mutually balanced tariff concessions was regarded as overly restrictive, and policies to increase imports over exports were advised. The U.S. State Department, which gained the upper hand over Congress on trade policy, wanted to *reduce* the American trade surplus after the war in order to relieve a dollar shortage abroad. In effect, it exhorted Americans to "Buy foreign." One report stated, "We have an unfavorable balance of trade, unfavorable to the taxpayer and unfavorable to the consumer. . . . We must become really import-minded" and "not fear that someone in the United States is going to be hurt."

A report prepared by a Board on Mutual Security in 1953 for President Truman recommended that the United States eliminate "unnecessary" protection for American industries producing automobiles, machinery, and consumer electronics such as radios and televisions. Because these industries were so advanced and efficient, "this country has nothing to fear." The report also favored lowering tariffs on industries such as textiles and apparel, with duties of 25 percent or more, in order to make way for a "substantial increase in imports."

Under the Republican administration of Dwight D. Eisenhower, strategic trade policy ratcheted up another notch. Eisenhower, a military man, was highly critical of the protectionist American business community, especially in labor-intensive industries, writing in his diary about its "shortsightedness bordering upon tragic stupidity": "To secure allied support for strategic export controls against the Soviet Union, the United States must provide alternative markets in the West." Eisenhower wanted a system of global trade that "allowed backward people to make a decent living—even if a minimum one measured by American standards." Otherwise, in the long run the United States would fall "prey to the communist attack."

Beginning in 1948 the United States "quietly" waived its rights under a number of bilateral trade agreements with developing countries—Brazil, Ceylon (Sri Lanka), Cuba, and Pakistan—and agreed to discrimination against American exports for balance-of-payments and development reasons. Discrimination against the American market was so widespread that, in 1950, the U.S. Tariff Commission found that "only 4 of the 42 countries with which the United States had bilateral trade agreements in force employed neither import licenses nor exchange controls." Nor were the four open economies heavy hitters. They were American neocolonies—Cuba, El Salvador, Guatemala, and Haiti.

In 1958, the American Chamber of Commerce asked the State Department for information about the products on which the United States had received tariff concessions and which were competitive with U.S. substitutes. The State Department offered some examples (office machines and typewriters for Germany, vitamins for Japan), but admitted that although "there must be many more such items," the research required to name them had not been done. In other words, "the State Department did not monitor the results of its negotiations," and lacked specific information for U.S. business about the benefits, if any, of liberalization.

President Kennedy was of the same mind as Truman and Eisenhower. In removing import barriers, he imagined that the United States could "act as a giant engine of economic development" for poor nations. In a 1963 speech he spoke of the "Atlantic responsibility" to open "our markets to the developing countries of Africa, Asia and Latin America."

The tide began to turn in 1968, when the Vietnam War destabilized the U.S. balance of payments. The presidential race of that year (won by Nixon) exposed alleged public frustration with nonreciprocal, one-sided trade liberalization. Still, the former chairman of the U.S. International Trade Commission concludes: "Japan and many of the other rapidly industrializing powers—Taiwan, South Korea, and Brazil among others—enjoyed rapid economic growth, not because they practiced free trade at home, but because they enjoyed access to the open American market."

In fact, the openness of the American market was grossly exaggerated. High tariffs in the United States, Europe, and Japan protected precisely those industries in which the developing countries supposedly had a comparative advantage: textiles and garments, shoes and other labor-intensive goods, iron and steel, and agricultural and mineral products. Tariffs on American textiles, a major exception and a leading domestic sector in the nineteenth century, began in 1812 and lasted until the present—*nearly 200 years!* Economists estimate that without protection (against the "Nannies" of Nanking, China, and the "Indies" of India after the American War for Independence), the U.S. textile industry would have collapsed (later at the hands of Japan), notwithstanding its easy access to southern raw cotton and its extraordinary technological inventiveness.[12]

Ironically, the greater openness of the American market for more capital-intensive and technologically advanced industries, such as chemicals, machinery, and nonferrous metals, helped the more precocious developing countries climb the ladder of comparative advantage and export using higher skills than otherwise. Industrialization in these countries was given the oxygen it desperately needed. The developing countries that were hurt the most were the poorest raw-material exporters—the flip side of comparative advantage.

In relative terms, how beneficent the First American Empire was! World growth under "redistributive" trade was unprecedented, especially in the Third World, including its poorest parts (see figure 1.1). Alas, as we'll soon see, the First Empire was too weak economically to sustain a nonreciprocal trade regime, especially when Europe and Japan recovered. The United States couldn't—and ultimately didn't—keep importing while the other richer countries of the world kept their markets shut. For a security model of imperialism to hold, an empire must enjoy extraordinary economic power, as well as strong support from its most advanced allies. The United States was strong, but not of mythological proportions, because it mishandled growth in its own backyard, the Americas.

VI "Talk and Talk"

The United States globalized trade after the war—bringing as many countries as possible into the same system—and cut a big slice of the pie for the Third World: "From its predominant position during the postwar years, the United States saw the development of a strong multilateral trading system as the most satisfactory means for defending its strategic interests and exercising political and economic leadership."[13]

The General Agreement on Tariffs and Trade (GATT) was established in 1947, and its productive life ended only when the hawkish World Trade Organization (WTO) replaced it in 1995. By comparison with the WTO, GATT was gentle and generous to developing countries, the product of a security-minded empire that bent with the wind rather than a pugnacious superpower that gave no ground. GATT members were not required to adhere to all GATT protocols; they could select only those they were able to follow. Freedom of choice made economic development far easier. There were also safeguards in GATT (stronger than in the WTO) that protected the nascent industries of weaker countries from wildly unstable markets and the cartels and monopolistic practices of developed countries. Imagine how difficult it would have been in the absence of GATT for the automobile industries of Korea, India, and China, for example, to compete initially against those of Japan, the United States, and Germany, which not only enjoyed long experience, loyal supplier networks, cash reserves, brand-name recognition, and technological prowess, but also the cheap labor of the low-wage countries (first in southern Europe) in which their plants were selectively located. With fresh new entrants, automobile consumers worldwide ultimately enjoyed more competition than ever before, and the developing countries with automobile sectors enjoyed more jobs and small-scale parts and components manufacturers (China, India, Korea, Thailand, Brazil, and Mexico). As the Enlightenment taught, competition is great, especially for countries that are growing.

Part of the clout that the United States exercised in GATT and the WTO, both big bureaucracies, derived from its professional, knowledgeable, experienced, and research-oriented public trade organizations, which functioned in Washington to advance U.S. interests abroad, whatever the posture of partisan politics at home. In the first round of tariff negotiations in GATT in 1948 (there were seven rounds in total, such as the Dillon

Round, the Kennedy Round, and finally, the Uruguay Round), the U.S. Tariff Commission prepared information on the 1,300 items on which the United States was willing to offer concessions, and 5 commissioners and 22 staff members went to Geneva to participate in the talks.[14] These talks were allegedly multilateral, but they shared much in common with America's bilateral trade negotiations from 1934 to 1945. The U.S. trade representatives had an edge over all other delegations with less experience.

In the negotiations, "a team from each country conducted the day to day bargaining with representatives of another nation (usually an important trading partner) on a bilateral basis." Once tariff concessions had been completed at the bilateral level, each country consolidated the concessions it had agreed upon into a single schedule that became part of the GATT. The first round of concessions took seven months to hammer out and dealt with 45,000 tariff items. This represented the largest multinational trade negotiations ever held up to that time, and it brought about striking reductions in the overall level of tariff barriers throughout the world, mostly in the United States and Europe.

The developing countries had nowhere near the United States's savvy in picking industries on which to offer concessions, in negotiating with potentially important trading partners, or in advancing the cause for freer trade in those commodities on which their lifeblood depended. The same was true of negotiations under the WTO. In fact, most developing countries still had no voice at all when GATT was founded; as colonies, they were appendages. The earliest members in GATT from the Third World were mostly from Latin America, where communist insurgency was far less in evidence at the time than in Asia, and whose political demands were blander.

Ironically, once they became independent, developing countries benefited from postwar bipartisan politics in the United States. Both Democrats and Republicans in Congress were uneasy about "globalism." Democrats feared a fall in the living standards of their working-class and minority constituents, while Republicans feared a loss in national sovereignty from international commitments. The two parties banded together to insist that any international trade agreement, present and future, have an "*escape clause*" provision, as found in some earlier bilateral trade agreements. The provision (Article XIX of GATT and Executive Order 9832 of the United States) protected U.S. producers against serious injury perpetrated by negotiated concessions. In such an event, the United States reserved the right to withdraw from a protocol, modify a concession, and/or exact compensation for an injury.

Escape clauses were a godsend for developing countries because they enabled them to opt out of protocols that endangered their fledgling industries. They could protect themselves from import surges, from imports that destabilized their balance of payments, and from unfair trade practices (Article VI on antidumping and countervailing duties). Over GATT's 50-year history, these escape clauses were invoked almost exclusively by *developed* countries. Nevertheless, developing countries also tenuously enjoyed "*special and differential treatment.*" This treatment enabled them to experience multilaterally what they had experienced bilaterally with the United States: *nonreciprocity*, or lower average tariffs than those of the developed world. For nearly half a century, most of the developing world's newest, modern industries were protected.

Despite what many free-market economists feared—a black hole of safeguards, special and differential treatment, and the cumbersome nature of negotiations (prompting them to rename GATT the "General Agreement to Talk and Talk")—GATT was highly successful in achieving its major goal: lower tariffs (see table 3.1). Even before the Uruguay Round, which GATT undertook at the instigation of the trade hawks, tariffs had fallen from their postwar rooftop level, especially in Europe, Japan, and the United States. Even the average tariffs of those developing countries squarely in the orbit of modern-world industry became pretty low, such as those of Korea, Thailand, Brazil, and Mexico. As table 3.1 shows, the exceptions were India, which had an average tariff of over 70 percent going into the Uruguay Round, and Indonesia, whose average tariff rose coming out of it.

Thus, by 1995 the tariffs of developing countries had become reasonable by any standard, even that of free trade. As the baton was handed to the WTO, its work *on tariffs* was nearly complete. Ironically, what remained was to get the United States, Europe, and Japan to lower their trade barriers as quickly as possible on textiles and especially agricultural goods, since the developing world was still struggling with hunger. The claim is widely accepted that "the GATT has made a valuable contribution to postwar economic growth, by stabilizing trade relations and promoting trade liberalization."[15] In fact, apart from trimming tariffs, GATT's greatest contribution to Third World development was arguably the very *opposite* of

Table 3.1
Trade-Weighted Tariff Averages before and after Liberalization (Pre- and Post-Uruguay Round)

	Pre-Uruguay	Post-Uruguay
Developing Countries		
Argentina	38.2%	30.9%
Brazil	40.7%	27.0%
Chile	34.9%	24.9%
India	71.4%	32.4%
Indonesia	20.4%	36.9%
Korea	18.0%	8.3%
Malaysia	10.0%	10.1%
Mexico	46.1%	33.7%
Thailand	37.3%	28.0%
Turkey	25.1%	22.3%
Developed Countries		
European Union	5.7%	3.6%
Japan	3.9%	1.7%
United States	5.4%	3.5%

The pre-Uruguay duties refer to 1994 bound duties or, for unbound tariff lines, to duties applicable as of September 1986. The post-Uruguay duties refer to the concessions listed in the schedules annexed to the Uruguay Round Protocol to the GATT 1994. Import statistics refer in general to 1988, so trade-weighted duties using post-Uruguay import data may be slightly different. The data are preliminary and may be revised to reflect the final schedules annexed to the Final Act of the Uruguay Round, although as of April 1999 no changes were registered except for Thailand. The changes for Thailand appear above.
Source: OECD, 1994, Appendix Tables 5 and 6.

liberalization—it allowed developing countries to deviate from the principles of free trade in order to build the modern industries they needed to trade at all. Without something to export, open markets have nothing inside.

VII Replication

Competition between communism and capitalism opened an unprecedented window of opportunity for developing countries to industrialize. The clash of ideas was nurturing. Neither the European empires of the prewar era nor the Second American Empire after 1980 came close to matching the economic growth that occurred when the Third World enjoyed *non*reciprocity. It got away with keeping its markets closed while gaining access to the markets America opened. It built its industries, which enabled it to trade more in the future. In this respect, Keynes's unorthodox ideas on trade were right.

Despite the brain trusts, Camelot, and the fact that no one "gave a damn" about what the Third World did, despite the counterthemes and unconventional thinking about free trade, the United States again and again proved itself to be a conservative country in foreign economic policy. The Third World was able to do whatever it wanted because of the conflicts and conventions of the time, not out of any strong conviction that the Royalists were wrong or that protection of infant industries was right.

Does this mean that planning and unconventional policies can never be replicated? When income differences between North and South are large—and on average, they're getting larger—there will always be a cold war and the need for a shrewd trade policy. The current conflict between the United States and China is a Cold War of sorts. The war against terrorism is also a Cold War because, in the name of religion, the terrorists represent the poor and the United States represents the rich. In the presence of global income inequalities, the South can't be held to the same policy standards as the North; otherwise it will find it extremely difficult to grow, at great social cost.

Trade was always a puny part of the American gross domestic product (GDP)—only 5 percent was exported from 1924 to 1928 and again in 1960. This share was almost as low as Russia's, 3 percent in 1959 and 1965 (as a percent of GNP). Now the GDP share of U.S. exports is between 10 percent and 15 percent, not a trivial amount, but still small enough to warrant experiment for world prosperity and peace.

4 Angel Dust

A Chinese proverb says, A fish lasts a day, but *knowledge* of fishing and a fishing rod last a lifetime. In fact, a fishing rod and knowledge are as useless as a fish unless a country's fishing industry has money to buy boats and nets, has finance to invest in canning facilities and freezing equipment, and has access to large enough markets to make fishing pay. These resources require coordination between aid, investment, infrastructure, and trade policy. Aid alone is a fish out of water.

I More Than Even a Rod to Fish

Aid was part of the First American Empire's experimental approach to economic development. Before this period, there had been no aid in the colonial world. Yet the American record in aid was weaker than that in trade, so the gap widened between poor developing countries dependent on aid and less poor developing countries able to export manufactures, the fastest-growing markets after the war. Besides the accusation of corruption, *aid lacked supporting and coordinating investment.* Aid to education is useless if the educated can't find jobs, and the creation of jobs requires investments in new industries. Otherwise, the precious few who are educated become part of the discontented or start a torrential brain drain. Clean water or sanitary plumbing is a dream come true for the informal sector, but even the self-employed can barely subsist unless they have loans large enough to modernize their trade. The exception that proves the rule is the Green Revolution, which provided farmers with the means to earn a livelihood in the long run, and not just with clean water and modern sewage. Without complementary capital, aid becomes an addiction.

The largest slice of the total American aid pie was dished up for Europe and Japan under the Marshall Plan (named after a speech at Harvard in 1947 by Secretary of State George Marshall). According to Paul Hoffman, the first administrator of the U.S. aid agency that oversaw the Marshall Plan, "We have learned in Europe what to do in Asia." Like Europe, Asia was a hot spot of communist insurgency, and fighting communism was the raison d'être of aid under the First American Empire. Yet what happened in Europe was never remotely replicated in the developing world, although Asia got a lot of military aid. There was talk of creating mini–Marshall Plans, and a multilateral super-aid organization within the United Nations. It was called SUNFED (Special United Nations Fund for Economic Development), but was soon dubbed "UNFED" because it never got off the ground.[1]

Poverty rates fell sharply over time, and the absolute amount of aid increased. In certain crises, like the Asian tsunami of 2005, aid demonstrated what it could do. After the defeat of SUNFED, the United Nations continued to give technical assistance and "multilateral" aid (from more than a single donor). The Scandinavian countries were major givers. Developing countries began offering aid to other developing countries, especially in the Arab world. But American aid never became the spark for human development that it was meant to be. Nor did aid and investment ever make their peace, except in some military projects. Over time, aid became a smaller share of government spending and GDP, spiking only when the cold war was at its hottest (see table 4.1)

Aid was political because it was controlled by Congress, and corruption by the recipients led to its ill repute. The major lesson from aid was learned by the Third World itself, which went on to struggle mostly on its own. Maybe that was the major purpose of aid in the first place.

II Money Can't Buy Love

Without proven technology and managerial expertise, firms from developing countries couldn't easily finance their industrialization. Investors were leery of lending to those short of know-how. But without finance, developing countries couldn't invest in developing expertise in the long term. Experienced enterprises in the North typically financed their investments with retained earnings, but this source of credit was unavailable to inexperienced

Table 4.1
United States Foreign Aid

	Foreign Aid as Share of Government Spending	Foreign Aid as Share of GDP
1945	2%	.8%
1946	3.5%	.8%
1947	16.8%	2.5%
1948	15.3%	1.7%
1949	15.6% Decade avg.: 10.64%	2.2% Decade avg.: 1.6%
1950	10.9%	1.6%
1951	8%	1.1%
1952	3.9%	.74%
1953	2.7%	.56%
1954	2.2%	.42%
1955	3.2%	.55%
1956	3.4%	.56%
1957	4.1%	.68%
1958	4%	.71%
1959	3.4% Decade avg.: 4.58%	.63% Decade avg.: .75%
1960	3.2%	.55%
1961	3.2%	.58%
1962	5.2%	.98%
1963	4.7%	.88%
1964	4.1%	.76%
1965	4.4%	.75%
1966	4.1%	.72%
1967	3.5%	.67%
1968	2.9%	.61%
1969	2.5% Decade avg.: 3.78%	.48% Decade avg.: .69%
1970	2.2%	.43%
1971	1.9%	.37%
1972	2%	.39%
1973	1.6%	.31%
1974	2.1%	.39%
1975	2.1%	.44%
1976	1.7%	.36%
1977	1.5%	.31%
1978	1.6%	.33%
1979	1.4% Decade avg.: 1.81%	.29% Decade avg.: .32%
1980	2.1%	.46%
1981	1.9%	.42%
1982	1.6%	.38%

Table 4.1
(continued)

	Foreign Aid as Share of Government Spending	Foreign Aid as Share of GDP
1983	1.4%	.34%
1984	1.8%	.41%
1985	1.7%	.38%
1986	1.4%	.32%
1987	1.1%	.24%
1988	.9%	.2%
1989	.8% Decade avg.: 1.57%	.17% Decade avg.: .33%
1990	1%	.23%
1991	1%	.26%
1992	1.1%	.25%
1993	1.2%	.26%
1994	1.1%	.24%
1995	1%	.22%
1996	.8%	.17%
1997	.9%	.18%
1998	.7%	.15%
1999	.8% Decade avg.: .96%	.16% Decade avg.: .21%
2000	.9%	.17%
2001	.8%	.16%
2002	1.1%	.21%

Source: Office of Management and Budget, *Fiscal Year 2005 Historical Tables of the U.S. Government.*

firms in the South, aside from a few excellent companies, like Tata of India, with a reputation for honesty and profitability, that could raise their own capital. When Tata made a stock offering, the rich were willing to invest their savings. Its new steel mill, the first in colonial India in 1909, was oversubscribed in a matter of days. In capital-intensive industries like steel, cement, petrochemicals, and pulp and paper, based on big investments in capital stock, "suppliers' credits" were available. Specialized suppliers of capital stock provided user industries with equipment and machinery and the credit to buy them. Diesel engines for ships, like Burmeister's of Denmark, might also come with credit attached. In the 1960s, suppliers' credits accounted for roughly one-fourth of developing countries' total capital formation. But the cost of this capital tended to be very high.

Until well into the 1980s, *no banks in the North lent to a private company in the South.* For fear of default, a "sovereign" guarantee of repayment was demanded. Governments had to come up with the cash if a loan fell into default, giving states huge power over the private investment process. Foreign direct investments by multinational firms were another potential bonanza, but accounted for a small share of total capital even in the 12 developing countries with prewar manufacturing experience. Net foreign direct investment as a share of gross domestic capital formation in 1975 to 1979 exceeded 5 percent only in Malaysia, which was rich in raw materials.[2]

The First American Empire made only a very limited number of soft loans available to private Third World enterprises, mainly small in scale. Private lending was left to the private sector. Loans to industry even by the World Bank were few and far between, although this was the Bank's mission stipulated at Bretton Woods. By around 2000, *only 17 percent* of the Bank's total loans had gone to the Third World's industrial sector and financial services. Countries had to look elsewhere for money to industrialize. When Korea was building its POSCO steel mill in the early 1970s, Korea twisted Japan's arm for colonial reparations. When India was building its Bokaro steel mill, it got finance from Russia, with disastrous results for its technology.

Raising capital was a big problem. Third World governments devoted themselves to this end and were judged by it. The most important source of finance was the transfer of resources from agriculture to industry. The amount transferred depended on rural productivity, tax rates, and the artificial price governments charged to farmers for fertilizers, often manufactured by publicly owned firms. The East Asian countries with land reforms that made agriculture more efficient—Korea, Taiwan, parts of India and Malaysia—got a jump at industrial financing.

In the 1970s, the inflow of petrodollars from oil-producing countries provided undreamt quantities of capital at cheap prices. Projects that had been on the drawing board for decades were begun. New industries mushroomed overnight. Big business expanded and reached economies of scale. But low-cost investment finance was like rain in a parched land: too much came in a short time, creating flood conditions in the absence of regulations. The land again became arid and lending ceased. But deregulation of financial markets and debt traps were the business of the Second American Empire.

III Tying the Knot

The Roosevelt and Truman administrations were the inventors of "aid," a new source of finance in the form of soft loans or outright grants to developing countries. As I've shown, aid was part of the American experiment. It was indispensable in emergencies like earthquakes, floods, and famines. It was humane in providing the needy with electricity, medicines, clean water, and modern sanitation. It was the warrior against poverty. But even the best of aid was subject to fatal flaws and became an "aid business."

One flaw of aid was corruption, a failure on the part of both donor and recipient that dead-ended in a huge waste of resources. Even U.S. aid to Taiwan and Korea in the 1950s, hailed as a model, was misallocated, with a large amount apparently used to finance the rise of private big business. In practice, these businesses became the backbone of East Asia's economy, but in principle, they gave aid a bad name. Ultimately, fighting corruption distracted a lot of angry donors.

On the other side of the coin, the United States was the instigator of "tying" aid: *it tied 80 percent of the value of every aid project to the purchase of American-made goods or services*. This enriched companies like Bechtel rather than countries like Botswana. According to a blue-ribbon Commission on International Development (1969) that reported to the President of the World Bank, Robert McNamara: "The United States started the trend toward pervasive tying and managed in the process to reduce considerably the adverse impact of its aid on its balance of payments. Other countries have, of course, been subject to corresponding balance-of-payments pressures as a result of U.S. tying, and their own tying has at least in part been defensive."[3]

With Buy American, tying reduces the flexibility of how aid can be spent and may overload projects with needless frills. Instead of building a dirt road to help Ghanaian farmers sell their crops in distant markets, for example, a paved, two-lane highway was built that provided income for big, capital-intensive American contractors. Tying prevents an aid recipient from shopping worldwide for the best bargain, and from building an experienced local cadre of executives, managers, and engineers, with the result that the real value of aid is lower than the nominal value.

The First American Empire's aid was a godsend. Aid that raised agricultural productivity increased tax revenues, which indirectly helped finance investments in industry. But was all aid to agriculture on the side of the angels?

IV AgrAid

As late as 1966, agriculture as a share of national income was around 30 percent or over in Argentina, Brazil, Chile, and Mexico; around 60 percent or over in Malawi, Nigeria, and Uganda; around 30 percent or over in Burma, South Korea, the Philippines, and Thailand; and 50 percent in India and Pakistan. Aid to agriculture was critical to provide a livelihood to millions of farmers. It was also essential to nurture industry, supplying it with savings, foodstuffs for urban workers, exports, inputs for industrial manufacturing, and demand for manufacturing output.

American aid to agriculture was especially problematic, although agricultural aid was central to the European success of the Marshall Plan. Why the difference? Food aid, including animal feed and fertilizers, accounted for 49 percent of Europe's procurements from the United States in the immediate postwar years. There was not much need, however, for formal tying, since the United States at the time was the only effective source of supply for many of the Marshall Plan's requirements.[4] By contrast, tying was central to American food aid to developing countries, with contrary effects.

Despite (or because of) the bountifulness of America's natural resources and high productivity in exploiting them, the price of U.S. farm produce was continually falling, and U.S. farmers tended to earn *less* on average than U.S. workers. (This was why economists in the Third World argued that industrialization was necessary for economic development.) To boost American farmers' incomes and win their votes, Washington bought the crops that farmers couldn't sell on the open market above a specified price. This led to huge surpluses of agricultural commodities in government storage, as supply raced ahead of demand. Eisenhower was president at the time and came from Kansas, a heavily agricultural state. His administration's solution was foreign agricultural "aid" (the Agricultural Trade Development and Assistance Act of 1954, or Public Law 480), in the form of sales of surplus agricultural commodities to poor countries in exchange for local currencies.

Sometimes poor countries benefited from PL 480 because they got food without having to earn the "hard" currencies of advanced countries to pay for it. But the results of this law were often catastrophic for the innocent, impoverished Third World farmers who were supposed to benefit. When the United States emptied its granary, agricultural prices almost always fell worldwide, whether for wheat, corn, cotton, or rice. Due to such dumping, farmers specializing in one of these crops thousands of miles away from Congress faced falling market prices for their output, and so, too, falling incomes. American rice aid to India had the side effect of impoverishing rice growers in Burma and Thailand. This perverse globalism was due to one country's market power.

Unlike the red revolution, the dream of socialists, or PL 480 agricultural aid, the hobbyhorse of the U.S. Congress, the Green Revolution was the inspiration of the American eastern establishment—the Rockefeller Foundation, the Ford Foundation, the State Department, and the Council on Foreign Relations (which in 1939 supplied two-thirds of the Rockefeller Foundation's trustees). Dean Rusk, a Rhodes scholar and later a tragic figure in the Vietnam War, was appointed president of the Rockefeller Foundation in 1952 when research on rice was just getting started; later, he would serve as secretary of state from 1961 to 1969 under Presidents Kennedy and Johnson. Under the Mutual Security Act of 1951, the U.S. government paid Cornell University to develop a new agricultural and research program at the University of the Philippines at Los Banos. The Philippines was selected by the Rockefeller Foundation as the venue for the International Rice Research Institute (IRRI), which it financed, because the Philippines had once been a U.S. colony, it hosted a large amount of American foreign investment, its military was battling a popular communist guerrilla movement in the countryside, and its political life was democratic (until Ferdinand Marcos rose to power in the early 1970s). The Green Revolution was squarely in the middle of America's elite security model: increasing the developing world's food supply was expected to defeat left-wing insurgency. To be sure, this ideal was tainted with avarice. Even while the Rockefeller Foundation focused its philanthropy on the Philippines, Esso (now Exxon), a Rockefeller oil subsidiary, couldn't resist building a fertilizer complex for rice and other crops "that undercut two projects already announced by Philippine companies, which terminated their projects after the Esso announcement."[5] Still, the Green Revolution succeeded because it had the backing and private money of America's Royalists, without the interference of Congress.

Any revolution in the use of land raises the issue of land distribution. But the Green Revolution did not redistribute land from rich to poor farmers, even though the fastest-growing developing countries taught the importance of land reform. The United States–mandated land reform in postwar Japan was an immense success in terms of raising yields. Korea and Taiwan, Japan's former colonies, engineered their own land reforms to rival those of North Korea and China. Land reform was also at the heart of the Chinese Communist Revolution and the Maoist revolution in North Korea. Vietnam mobilized popular support for a land reform, and Bengal, a stronghold of the local Indian Communist Party, succeeded in redistributing land to the poorest peasants. Other developing countries, such as Egypt and the Philippines, tried their hands at equalizing land holdings with little success. Mexico broke up big estates after its revolution in 1910, but the need for renewed land reforms in later years indicates that redistribution was continually reversed.

Despite its successes, land reform became feared by the First American Empire because it was typically the brainchild of leftist political forces. Instead of instituting land reform in Vietnam, the United States airdropped thousands of leaflets over North Vietnam under the banner, "South Vietnam Is Experiencing a Rice Revolution." The Green Revolution was indeed akin to a rice revolution. The eradication of poverty through Green Revolution technology depended on the specific ecology and culture of a farming region. Irrigation was necessary to cultivate new rice strains, but roughly two-thirds of the world's poorest rice-growing regions were not yet irrigated. Who got the Green Revolution technology depended partly on luck.

The Green Revolution brought a *technology package* to the tropics. In diffusing modern technology to solve agricultural problems, it was in keeping with the times. By 1960, it was widely believed that technology could solve social problems, such as the developing world's population explosion (in 1952, the Rockefellers founded the Population Council, which emphasized contraceptive birth control). The global diffusion of Green Revolution technology, the transfer of knowledge from American scientists to local scientists, and the key role played in research and diffusion by Third World governments all helped to breathe life into the rural regions of the poorest countries.

Aid from Russia and China was also science-based, although traditional technology—for the Tanzania-Zambia railroad, for example—was also employed. Chinese scientists, working for the military, first discovered an herbal drug to treat malaria, which was supplied to Vietnamese troops fighting in the Mekong Delta.

Cross-breeding of plants had long been practiced in the temperate zones; it was an integral part of imperialism. A high-yielding rice, *japonica,* raised incomes in Japan and Taiwan, but this rice strain was unsuitable for the tropics, where *indica* was needed. Wheat-growing in Mexico was first to be revolutionized. Starting in 1940, wheat yields in Mexico's Sonora state nearly doubled in a decade. Plant-breeding had been conducted by Mexicans and Americans under the joint sponsorship of the Mexican government and the Rockefeller Foundation, drawing on knowledge from American land-grant colleges and federal experimental stations dating to the 1860s. But after World War II, the Rockefeller Foundation wanted to increase the productivity of rice especially, since it was the staple of nearly two-thirds of the world's poor, who lived in lands most vulnerable to communist takeover.

At the heart of the Green Revolution was the scientific breeding of varieties of high-yield rice. These types of rice were designed to respond positively to the use of chemical or natural fertilizers, thus producing more output per acre than otherwise. Local production of fertilizers provided an opportunity to establish a new industry with significant employment effects. In the 1960s, fertilizers for farmers became relatively cheap.

Compared with the revolution in genetically modified (GM) foods forty years later, the Green Revolution had one virtue—it was not for profit. The GM revolution, according to *Scientific Magazine* (August 2004), is dominated by big corporations who want profits from modifying the mass production crops of rich countries. GM plants can't be reseeded, whereas Green Revolution plants can. Consequently, farmers using GM plants must buy expensive new seeds each year, whereas farmers using hybrid plants need not do so.

For higher yields, new rice strains under the Green Revolution demanded scientific farming. Irrigation had to be timed properly. Fertilizers and insecticides had to be applied in the right amounts. Learning required attention and experimentation, and no single formula fit all ecologies. By 1976, IRRI had trained 1,600 production specialists, mostly from India, Pakistan, and Bangladesh. Most of IRRI's staff was also Asian, although senior scientists and IRRI's director remained American. Arguably, however, "lateral" learning was most important: "New seeds, information, labour, tools, and credit were transferred, exchanged, borrowed, and given from neighbor to neighbor and kinsman to kinsman far more often than any transfer from the district agricultural officer to the extension worker to the farmer."

The Green Revolution mainly helped the large farmer. It also created only minimal employment for the landless. But after a quarter of a century, *the food production problem of the developing world had been solved, and the incomes of millions of farmers had risen.* The UN's Millennium Task Force on Hunger and Nutrition (2000) found little starvation, mostly *owing to low levels of output on a national scale.* Hunger and malnutrition still abounded, of course. But they were due to distribution, not production. If anything, farmers suffered from falling prices due to oversupply.

The Green Revolution was the takeoff for industry, and the United States was behind it all.

V DefAid

The developing countries that got the most aid were not necessarily the poorest countries. In the late 1980s, about 40 percent of external assistance was given to middle- and high-income countries "largely for political reasons," as close an estimate as possible to the share of military aid in total aid.[6] National security sometimes required the United States to give aid for nonmilitary ends. Did defense aid, known as DefAid, have anything to do with economic development?

Immediate postwar U.S. military aid policies toward East Asia and Latin America emphasized the build-up of conventional weapons to withstand an *external* attack. When the cold war started, the United States and Latin America signed the Rio Pact to guarantee hemispheric solidarity against Soviet aggression. The Mutual Security Act prepared the way for the United States to assist Latin America in modernizing its armed forces. The United States sent it patrol boats and reconnaissance aircraft, fearing a submarine or naval attack in the South Atlantic.

The other side of the planet was no different. Taiwan was given weapons ranging from guns to helicopters to deter Chinese aggression, but U.S. policies began to change in Korea, when the American and Korean militaries joined forces in 1948 to purge the Korean army of communists (Park Chung Hee, who led a coup in 1961 and set Korea on a path of ultrarapid

Table 4.2
United States Military Spending

	Military Spending as Share of Government Spending	Military Spending as Share of GDP
1945	89.5%	37.5%
1946	77.3%	19.2%
1947	37.1%	5.5%
1948	30.6%	3.5%
1949	33.9% Decade avg.: 53.7%	4.8% Decade avg.: 14.1%
1950	32.2%	5.0%
1951	51.8%	7.3%
1952	68.1%	13.2%
1953	69.4%	14.1%
1954	69.5%	13.0%
1955	62.4%	10.8%
1956	60.2%	9.9%
1957	59.3%	10.1%
1958	56.8%	10.2%
1959	53.2% Decade avg.: 58.3%	10.0% Decade avg.: 10.4%
1960	52.2%	9.3%
1961	50.8%	9.3%
1962	49.0%	9.2%
1963	48.0%	8.9%
1964	46.2%	8.5%
1965	42.8%	7.4%
1966	43.2%	7.7%
1967	45.4%	8.8%
1968	46.0%	9.4%
1969	44.9% Decade avg.: 46.8%	8.7% Decade avg.: 8.7%
1970	41.8%	8.1%
1971	37.5%	7.3%
1972	34.3%	6.7%
1973	31.2%	5.9%
1974	29.5%	5.5%
1975	26.0%	5.5%
1976	24.1%	5.2%
1977	23.8%	4.9%
1978	22.8%	4.7%
1979	23.1% Decade avg.: 29.4%	4.6% Decade avg.: 5.8%
1980	22.7%	4.9%
1981	23.2%	5.1%
1982	24.8%	5.7%

Table 4.2
(continued)

	Military Spending as Share of Government Spending	Military Spending as Share of GDP
1983	26.0%	6.1%
1984	26.7%	5.9%
1985	26.7%	6.1%
1986	27.6%	6.2%
1987	28.1%	6.1%
1988	27.3%	5.8%
1989	26.5% Decade avg.: 25.9%	5.6% Decade avg.: 6.4%
1990	23.9%	5.2%
1991	20.6%	4.6%
1992	21.6%	4.8%
1993	20.7%	4.4%
1994	19.3%	4.1%
1995	17.9%	3.7%
1996	17.0%	3.5%
1997	16.9%	3.3%
1998	16.2%	3.1%
1999	16.2% Decade avg.: 19%	3.0% Decade avg.: 4%
2000	16.5%	3.0%
2001	16.4%	3.0%
2002	17.3%	3.4%
2003	17.6% (estimate)	3.5%
2004	17.5% (estimate)	3.5%

Source: Office of Management and Budget, *Fiscal Year 2005 Historical Tables of the U.S. Government.*

growth, had been trained in the Tokyo Military Academy and became a member of the Japanese Communist Party). Then in 1951 civil war broke out and the United States and South Korea, under the United Nations' banner, fought against the northern invasion, along much the same lines that it fought the Axis powers in World War II. *Forty-five thousand* American soldiers died.

The rise of Fidel Castro changed the direction of warfare. The thrust of U.S. military assistance shifted from concern over an attack from *without* to concern over rebellion from *within*. Under the Kennedy Administration, the emphasis in military strategy became fighting domestic unrest. According to the Pentagon, this strategy involved "those military, paramilitary, political, economic, psychological, and civic actions taken by a government to defeat subversive insurgency," which during the Cold War the United States almost always associated with the political left.[7] In a speech at West Point in 1962, Kennedy stated: "Subversive insurgency is another type of war, new in its intentions, ancient in its origins—war by guerrillas, subversives, insurgents, assassins, war by ambush instead of by combat, by infiltration instead of aggression; seeking victory by eroding and exhausting the enemy instead of engaging him.... It requires ... a whole new kind of strategy, a wholly different kind of force, and therefore a new and wholly different kind of training."

The new mission required that counterinsurgency forces become more deeply and intimately involved in a country's political and economic life, which altered the nature of aid tying. American military aid to developing countries had always been conventionally "tied." A naval mission to Brazil during World War II, for example, insisted on the "predominance of the U.S. in Brazilian and Western Hemisphere affairs." In addition, Brazil had to introduce the use of United States material in the Brazilian Navy "in order to promote American trade."[8] But as counterinsurgency entangled the military more and more in economic development, tied aid came to mean *the tying of projects for economic development with projects for internal military security*. The border between them blurred.

In Thailand, military aid and rural development aid became indistinguishable, as the United States came to regard Thailand as a bulwark against communism in Vietnam. Thailand's own early development plans aimed to industrialize its country using United Nations technical assistance and European "bilateral aid" (involving one donor and one recipient), to counteract American influence. Thailand's central government also targeted the poorest provinces, in the northeast, for investments in infrastructure, especially transport, irrigation, and to a lesser extent health, education, and welfare. The focus of U.S. nonmilitary aid to all of Thailand became similar. But soon American aid was concentrated exclusively on the northeast region because insurgency was reported in 12 of its 16 provinces. The American military presence in Thailand expanded rapidly in the 1960s, and major bases to attack Vietnam were located in the northeast. Additionally, American military personnel were involved in a Northeastern Communist Suppression Command. Rural development was seen as an adjunct to counterinsurgency, and joint Thai-American northeastern rural development schemes were started in the mid 1960s with a large component of anticommunist, psychological education. The American ambassador to Thailand, General "Wild Bill" Donovan, brought with him 200 CIA advisers from Miami, seventy-six special operations military advisers, and around 500 members of other clandestine services.

The connection between rural development aid and counterinsurgency aid was even closer in war-torn South Vietnam, where whole villages were relocated to avoid communist takeover. In this case, both counterinsurgency and rural development failed.

Fighting subversives meant investing more in *indigenous* military, paramilitary, and police force training with the capacity to suppress any internal political unrest. By 1968, 76 percent of military aid to Latin America was for equipment or training related to counterinsurgency. The importance of training was emphasized by Robert McNamara in testimony before the House Appropriations Committee in 1962: "Probably the greatest return on our military assistance investment comes from the training of selected officers and key specialists at our military schools and training centers in the United States and overseas. These students are handpicked by their countries to become instructors when they return home. They are the coming leaders, the men who will have the know-how and impart it to their forces. I need not dwell upon the value of having in positions of leadership men who have first-hand knowledge of how Americans do things and how they think. It is beyond price to us to make such friends of such men."[9]

In the decade of 1959 to 1969, the United States trained an average of 3,475 Latin American military personnel each year. Between 1964 and 1968 alone, 22,059 men received instruction. Training in such courses as jungle operations, urban counterinsurgency, and military intelligence interrogation occurred at the U.S. Army School of the Americas in the Panama Canal Zone (where the United States ultimately overthrew the Noriega government) and at the Inter-American Defense College in Washington, D.C.

In the final analysis, the results of the First American Empire's *military* aid to developing countries was mixed. After the capture in Bolivia in 1967 of Che Guevara, Fidel Castro's comrade-in-arms, there was no major, sustained leftist uprising in Latin America. This is extraordinary, given the area's abject poverty and unequal income distribution, with wealth concentrated in a few families. Although income distribution in Latin America was among the most unequal in the world, the United States did nothing to change it, and possibly even increased it. American anticommunist counterinsurgency south of the border achieved its goal.

In Asia, communist guerrillas were defeated in Malaysia, the Philippines, Indonesia, and Thailand. In Taiwan and South Korea, communism was destroyed through aid and bloody war. But whatever successes the United States had in East Asia, its failure in Vietnam was catastrophic, and brought a whole era, including the First American Empire, down with it.

The economic spillover of defense aid was probably mildly positive. The boom in demand from the Korean War helped Thailand and Pakistan sell their rice, and helped a war-devastated Japan recover. The Supreme Commander of the Allied Forces in the Pacific (SCAP), responsible for supplying the armies in Korea, gave a big contract for electronic devices to the Sony Corporation, later one of Japan's premier electronics giants (when SCAP first approached Sony, its managers were sitting at their desks under umbrellas because of a leaky roof). Korea's major business group, Hyundai, got its start providing automobile repair services to the American army after the Korean War ended in 1953. Later, Hyundai accumulated construction know-how working for American forces in Vietnam. This experience was transferred to Hyundai's operations in the Middle East when demand for construction services soared during the oil boom of the 1970s. Middle Eastern demand led Hyundai to establish subsidiaries to manufacture cement and heavy earth-moving equipment. In Thailand, military aid to the northeast generated the rise of service industries, greater urbanization, and improved transportation.

Wars require big bureaucracies, and these survived in peacetime. In Japan, such bureaucracies waged a full-scale war for economic development. T. Hikino notes: "Allied powers needed the quick recovery of Japan's economy so that communist aggression did not spread further in Japan and the rest of East Asia. Bureaucratic organs that had directed wartime mobilization were thus revitalized for peacetime reconstruction and development. The Ministry of Finance (MOF) and the Ministry of International Trade and Industry (MITI) became the focal point of economic management."[10]

The militaries in Vietnam, Thailand, Malaya, Taiwan, and South Korea were all coherent and disciplined hierarchies, and hence "modernizers," as Samuel P. Huntington argued.[11] All played a major role in taking a nationalist approach to development. But militaries in other parts of the world failed miserably as modernizers and fought viciously for the status quo.

VI A Failed Experiment

The policy pronouncement of President Franklin Roosevelt favoring "trade, not aid" was prophetic. What helped the developing world industrialize were the open-ended trade policies described in the last chapter, not the tight-fisted aid policies described in this chapter. With the exception of the Green Revolution, which circumvented Congress, aid became a business. Through tying, American business was treated preferentially and not always transparently for aid-financed jobs. Although aid didn't support Third World business, corruption created a nouveau riche class that sometimes invested in business. Still, tying precluded the acquisition of engineering and managerial experience that developing countries most needed.

Americans, Japanese, and Europeans—aside from the Scandinavian countries—became less and less willing to sacrifice their tax dollars for aid, except for disaster relief. Aid's share in American GDP was highest right after the war (due to the Marshall Plan) and then fell steadily over time (see table 4.1). By the year 2000, billions of dollars were still being fought over, but aid's share was paltry—*Americans were sacrificing less than one-fifth of one percent of their GDP for poor countries*. Congressional lobbying in the United States and robbing the till in the Third World made aid countercultural.

Foreign aid was like the hallucinogen called angel dust—it felt good, but it had a lot of bad side effects. Most developing countries never got hooked on it and, thanks to the First American Empire, could go their own way.

5 Gift of the Gods

Few things are harder to put up with than the annoyance of a good example.

Mark Twain

I Know Thyself

The First American Empire's interpretation of laissez-faire as "do it your way" was a godsend to the Third World. Developing countries could be risk takers, trying out new institutions to industrialize. Their own knowledge could be put to use, whereas under the colonial "color bar" it was disparaged. As a result, the economic experiments of developing countries became historically unique. Although U.S. tariff rates were the highest in the world at the end of the nineteenth century, tariffs became part of a creative system of incentives and conditionalities in Third World development. In the best cases, protection was tightly tied to performance standards. Ideally, no incentive was given away for free. With performance standards, prosperity was no longer "just around the corner." It stared tens of countries and thousands of people in the face. The East Asian miracle's example grabbed the world's attention and goaded free market theory.

Central planning dated to around 1917, the year of the Russian Revolution, but most Third World countries never went as far as the Soviet Union or China in flouting market forces. Instead, they mixed market and state to varying degrees. The German National Socialist Party during World War II had both planning and industrial policies, and grew at record rates. But the Nazis' objectives were to save civilian labor for the army and to mobilize for war. By contrast, developing countries were interested in expanding the civilian labor force and investing in industries for commercial war. Japan was the first country to assign heavy weight to industrial policies, converting certain wartime institutions for peacetime use. Although Japan was the pioneer par excellence, developing countries varied Japan's industrial policies to create something qualitatively new. "Do it your way" liberated the spirit of the developing world as never before or since.

Import-substitution industrialization and its offspring, manufactured exports, lay at the heart of the Third World's experimentation. Manufacturing growth rates for roughly three decades after World War II were stunning on every continent, including Africa. This was the Golden Age of capitalism, which has since been forgotten, rationalized, ridiculed, and rejected. Mark Twain could have been speaking about today's Royalists when he said, "Few things are harder to put up with than the annoyance of a good example."

II Present at the Creation

The huge task of economic development fell on the shoulders of Third World nationals. The initiative to move from underdevelopment to development was not taken by multinational firms, or international banks, or U.S. technical assistants, or the State Department, or USAID, or American economists, no matter how much each portrayed itself retrospectively as a catalyst. Whatever role these foreign agents ultimately played, whatever influence the Bretton Woods institutions eventually had (World Bank lending to the Third World was anemic until at least 15 years after its foundation), they were not the first risk takers. Nor were the bushwhackers, or former collaborators of colonial rulers—the traditional tribal chiefs, princes, plantation managers, or import-export merchants. Traders (called "indentors" or "compradors" in China) preferred earning profits from importing rather than from investing locally in ventures that might displace imports; they were usually *opponents* of industrialization.[1] Instead, the movers and shakers, the new, foreign-educated cadre of risk takers, public and private, were rich families, business managers, teachers, distributors, retailers, technocrats, and other professionals who had felt the constraints of colonialism but who were conversant with Western ideas. Most major industries after World War II were established by nationally owned firms rather than by foreign holdings.[2]

The new elite was partly a reflection of colonialism's spread of "Western civilization" and partly the product of thousands of years of indigenous civilization in countries with long written histories, such as China, India, Indonesia, and Siam. The elite included the likes of Mahatma Gandhi, who was educated in London as a lawyer. Ho Chi Minh, the son of a mandarin, was a ship's steward who traveled from Saigon to Marseilles, and then spent time in France painting fake vases. Inspired by Woodrow Wilson, Ho argued for Vietnamese liberation at the Versailles peace conference in 1919, only to be shown the door. In 1945, he justified political independence for Vietnam by quoting the American Declaration of Independence. Fidel Castro, the son of rich landowners and the husband of one of the richest, was trained by the Jesuits. Zhou Enlai, communist China's dapper foreign minister, attended Japanese and Western missionary schools and later studied in Paris. Singapore's Lee Kuan Yew majored in law in Cambridge, U.K. Sukarno, Indonesia's father of independence, attended Dutch primary and secondary schools. Park Chung Hee, Korea's developmental president, learned the ways of the world by attending a Japanese military academy and joining the local communist party, as noted earlier. The king of Thailand, Rama IX, born in Cambridge, Mass., was educated in Switzerland. Mahathir Mohamad of Malaysia went to an English school where he received top honors in writing. Ramon Magsaysay, Philippine president for most of the 1950s, was the son of a teacher and blacksmith.

Africa tells more or less the same middle-class story. Nelson Mandela, the grandfather of independence worldwide, followed his father, councilor to a tribal chief, in studying law. Wole Soyinka, Nigeria's Nobel literature laureate (1986), was a political activist whose mother was a shopkeeper and whose father was headmaster of a primary school. Jomo Kenyatta attended a Scottish mission school and then, in the 1930s, studied at the London School of Economics under the famous anthropologist Branislaw Malinowski, publishing his thesis, *Facing Mount Kenya*, in 1938. Kwame Nkrumah, son of a goldsmith and father of Ghanaian independence, went to the United States in 1935 for advanced studies, which he continued in England, where he also worked to form a Pan-African Congress. Léopold Senghor, Senegal's first modern statesman, went to a Catholic school and then to the Sorbonne, where he developed the political and cultural movement of *négritude*. Julius Nyerere, who unified Zanzibar and Tanganyika, had a more unusual background. He was the son of a chief, but received an advanced degree in history and economics in the United Kingdom. Hastings Banda, first prime minister of Malawi (formerly Nyasaland), was a

U.S.-trained physician who later practiced medicine in Scotland. Patrice Lumumba, the fiery liberationist of the Congo, attended a Protestant mission school. Eddison Zvobgo, one of the leaders of the Zimbabwe National Union, was a Harvard-trained lawyer. Idi Amin, Uganda's murderous dictator, was unusual among these African leaders: he had little formal education and joined the British Colonial Army at an early age, participating in its repression of the Mau Mau rebellion.

Leadership in the Middle East and northern Africa was also international. Tunisian president Habib Bourguiba was the son of an army general who studied in a French *lycée.* Mohammed Mossadegh, Iran's democratically elected socialist leader overthrown by the CIA, was educated in England. Reza Pahlavi, who was involved in Mossadegh's overthrow and who became the shah with American connivance, studied in Switzerland. Even the Ayatollah Khomeini, after expulsion from Iraq in 1978 by Saddam Hussein, lived in exile for a year in France rather than in a Muslim country.

But not all independence leaders were cosmopolitan. Gamal Abdel Nasser, born poor in Alexandria, studied at a local military academy. David Ben-Gurion, born in Poland, went to a Hebrew school founded by his father, an ardent Zionist. Saddam Hussein studied at the University of Cairo's Law School. Algeria's Houari Boumédienne attended a university in Cairo and an Islamic institute at Constantine.

Although not all Western-trained leaders were knowledgeable about Western ways, by comparison with the politicians who ruled after 1980—virtually all of whom studied in the United States—the educations of the postwar independence heroes were more diverse geographically and intellectually. Starting in the 1980s, business schools would add more conformity to the education of political leaders. Nevertheless, all those who led their nation down the road to independence and economic development tended to know more about the West than the West knew about them.

III Leaving It Behind

The icons of colonial independence inspired hundreds of millions of people to sacrifice and save in the name of development. But the devil lay in the details. No matter how hands-on a political leader (Korea's Park Chung Hee, for one), most left industrialization to professional civil servants in government bureaucracies and professional managers in private firms. Most professionals were no-nonsense engineers. Their first foray into development planning was coming to terms with David Ricardo's great law of comparative advantage. This law held a clue to both underdevelopment in the past and development in the future.

During the first Industrial Revolution, spinning and weaving were the main industries, providing England with opportunities for entrepreneurship, mass employment, and machinery building. The longevity of England's textile industry is a marvel, but its conqueror, Japan, held court for nearly a century. Japan's silk and cotton textile industries eviscerated cotton spinning and weaving in Lancashire, the center of Britain's textile industry, because Japan excelled in production engineering, project execution, labor management, and attention to detail throughout the value chain. These skills were difficult for competitors to learn and emulate. In order to compete against Japan after World War II, the textile industries in other Third World countries, including Japan's former colonies, Korea and Taiwan, strayed from what is taught on comparative advantage in the best textbooks.

By the time the Third World was ready to focus on textiles, the industry may have become even more competitive than in the nineteenth century. In the same sector within the textile industry, low-wage countries battled high-skilled countries. Table 5.1 shows the export shares of garments and textiles from developed and developing countries in 2001 to 2002. In some of the largest segments, textile yarns and cotton fabrics, developed

Table 5.1
Who Exports Labor-Intensive Textiles? 2001–2002

	Developed Countries	Developing Countries
Textile yarn	45%	53%
Cotton fabrics	45%	54%
Woven man-made fibers	43%	56%
Knitted fabrics	35%	64%
Textile articles	35%	64%
Pharmaceutical products	93%	6%

Source: United Nations Conference on Trade and Development, *Trade and Development Report*, 2004.

countries still controlled a large market share—as much as 45 percent—excluding the exports of developed countries from outsourcing. News reports in the North emphasize factory closures and plants moving to developing countries, yet developing countries are depressed by the large amount of production that remains in the North—whatever happened to comparative advantage?

Industrial countries like France, Germany, Italy, and the United Kingdom could hold their own in labor-intensive industries because of automation, low-paid immigrant labor, brand names, and years of experience and know-how, most of which the law of comparative advantage assumes will not matter. The knowledge deficiency was most obvious in Korea. As early as the 1950s, when Korea was already exporting plywood and human wigs, it had everything it needed to enter textiles: production experience from Japan, low-paid female workers, martial law to repress trade union demands, new textile machinery financed by USAID, a well-educated population, and relatively advanced physical infrastructure. All this made Korea exceptionally competitive, in theory. *Yet Korea could still not compete against the mighty Japanese textile industry at market prices.* Costs of production were too high because productivity was too low.

Thus began Korea's adventures with industrial policy and government economic intervention to raise productivity through learning, and to bring the law of comparative advantage into line with modern times. Until Korean productivity rose enough, or Japan's wages rose enough, Korea's textile industry, a potential cash cow, was outflanked. To begin with, domestic production became protected and Korean firms became safe from Japanese takeovers. The same approach taken in textiles was taken in virtually every industry up the ladder of comparative advantage.

The players in raising productivity included machinery vendors, who taught Koreans how to improve the speeds and feeds of equipment and maintain old machinery, which was used when demand was high. Also, foreign consultants helped to improve the mixing of raw cotton and the rapid changeover to the types of yarns and fabrics that came into vogue. Finally, the government established a textile department at Seoul National University. Without these sources for know-how, Korea's wages would have had to become *negative* in order to compete. As productivity increased, and as Japan's wages rose during its growth-doubling decade of the 1960s, Korea's textile industry came alive. This was probably a longer, more circuitous, and more statist road to comparative advantage than David Ricardo ever imagined.

As the prestigious Pearson Commission observed more generally in its study of the Third World in the 1960s: "the American and European markets are ones in which *the less-developed countries' price advantage alone is usually not sufficient without detailed knowledge*."[3] The shortcoming of low wages was the starting point for a revision of comparative advantage and the design of government industrial promotion.

IV Heaven's Handiwork

Third World countries created their development institutions at roughly the same time. The "winds of change" that were blowing away imperialism were buffeting the whole developing world. Independence, nationalism, socialism, Keynesianism, and developmentalism were all in the air, in the newspapers, and in people's minds.

What arose like clockwork were systems to promote skill-intensive industries. In Thailand, a coup brought a general to power with private-business sympathies. A Promotion of Industrial Investment Act in 1960 created a Board of Investment that quickly began strengthening manufacturing activity. In Malaysia, a Pioneer Industry Ordinance of 1958 sparked industrial promotion that then intensified after race riots in 1969. In Indonesia, a new military government that came to power in 1966 under General Suharto started the long road to industrialization using many institutions established by the deposed leftist president Sukarno. In Korea, industrialization accelerated after a coup in 1961 and the rise to power of Park Chung Hee, the closest approximation in the Third World to "the great man of history." A planning ministry was tied to former Japanese banks to begin the process of designing mid-tech industries. In Taiwan, the Third Development Plan (1961–1964) emphasized the need to promote heavy industry, and with the formation of an Industrial Development Bureau in 1970, major investment projects accelerated. In India, Parliament passed an Industrial Policy Resolution in 1956 that triggered intense efforts to restructure existing industries and mostly to diversify into new basic manufacturing sectors. In Turkey, a 1960 coup led to the establishment of a State Planning Office and the start of Turkish postwar industrial expansion. In Brazil, the promotion of basic industries was the cornerstone of modernizing ideology and economic development. It started in the 1940s and raced ahead under President Kubitschek's "Target Plan" in the 1950s, which included an elite development bank. In Chile, the reconstitution of a development corporation in 1961 (CORFO) was the fillip behind more intensive industrial promotion. In Mexico, President Miguel Alemán made industrialization his *only* economic goal and, along with a "new group" of progressive industrialists, launched a vigorous plan to bolster manufacturing activity. Even China, with the least tolerance for market forces and an entirely different political economy, intensified its attempts at industrialization in 1958 with its Great Leap Forward.

Argentina was the sad exception—nothing much progressed there organizationally in the late 1950s or early '60s. Juan Perón's corrupt banks and nepotistic public agencies, dating from the 1940s or earlier, "crowded out" the professionally managed developmental machinery that arose in other countries. In the 1950s, the government of Arturo Frondizi adopted the nagging American policy of welcoming foreign investment, but foreign investors never provided strong leadership for diversification. As bureaucratic machinery in other countries began to grind away, Argentina's once-rich economy atrophied.

Although not nearly as industrialized as Argentina, the Philippines had a similar story. No developmental machinery was created, and the state's role was among the smallest in the Third World (the United States ruled from 1898 to 1946, and defeated a communist insurgency in the early 1950s). The economics Nobel laureate Gunnar Myrdal referred to the Philippines as a "soft state," because its bureaucracies were corrupt due to patronage and the wealthy in the plantation economy evaded paying taxes. Growth had the benefit of education, but this was much different from modern managerial skills.

V Budget Busters

After a short spending spree financed by the windfalls of war, the Third World's foreign exchange became extremely scarce. Solving this problem involved the governments' traditional macroeconomic ministries, especially the ministry of finance, as well as the new generation of bureaucracies related to industrial policy. In 1950, the Third World's dollar value of exports and imports were about equal. By 1960, imports exceeded exports by over ten percent, with no obvious way to pay for the shortfall (multinational investment favored only a few developing countries, mainly those rich in raw materials or with dynamic domestic markets). The traditional market remedy to balance-of-payments deficits was to let wages fall and thereby allow labor-intensive exports to increase. But to end the deficits, developing states would have had to let wages fall until they were *negative*. Instead, they tried something new, and some succeeded stupendously.

In the absence of tariffs, a typical balance-of-payments buster was the family of air conditioners, TVs, sewing machines, and the "whites" (refrigerators, stoves, and washing machines). Air conditioners were a blessing to the tropics, where summer temperatures in India, for example, might reach over 40°C, but however much they might help people work harder, they were originally a luxury import, preferred over locally made electric fans by those enjoying electric power. Television imports were also a big-ticket item, prized for the foreign news and entertainment they provided in cities and electrified villages. In 1971, a TV in a typical developing country cost about 12 times more than a radio.

In the family of transportation equipment, payments deficits were worse. To grow, countries needed trucks and tractors to move materials, vans for businesses, and buses, scooters, and bicycles to transport people. Demand for cars was growing among the elite by the 1960s. As imports of internal combustion engines climbed, the balance of payments was imperiled (especially if refined oil had to be imported as well). In desperation, governments tried to assemble locally imported "kits" of automobile parts and components, but sometimes importing the kits of a car cost more than importing the finished product. As local demand skyrocketed for the new, exciting consumer durables of the 1950s, deficits in the Third World's balance of payments worsened.

There are two ways to reduce the foreign exchange gap: export more, or substitute domestic production for imports. The latter, *import-substitution industrialization (ISI)*, provided a roadmap to entrepreneurs of what products were in local demand. If something was imported, someone wanted it. Governments provided state-owned enterprises and private-owned enterprises (SOEs and POEs) with tariffs and cheap finance to make import-substitution investments feasible. Then they offered other incentives to improve efficiency and product design. Later, they introduced still different incentives to convert import substitutes into exports.

Import substitution increased output, saved foreign exchange, and came to represent a prosperous era of industrial transformation in a newly politically independent Third World. It was during this Golden Age of import substitution that developing countries enjoyed the fastest growth rate in their history (see figure 1.1). Later, when ISI was under attack, most of the industries it spawned in the most advanced developing countries survived the opening of free trade. *The Third World's most common industries to fail under the laissez-faire policies of the Second American Empire were labor-intensive*, because these products suffered from the most brutal competition (soon from China). Hence, the high unemployment of the post-liberalization years had nothing to do with import substitution in advanced industries; import substitution was simply satanized by the Royalists to the point of irrationality, because the route taken to comparative advantage was roundabout and it threatened their own industries.

The virtue of exporting over import-substituting had a logic to it. By manufacturing *at free-market prices* those products that required inputs widely available locally (raw materials and labor), efficiency was maximized and exporting could be begun at once. Under import substitution, by contrast, efficiency failed in the short run because *any* import could be produced and sold locally if its tariff protection was high enough (like American-made textiles, which sparked industrialization but were protected for 200 years, and never really exported). This was the powerful counter-argument against import substitution that was heard on the sidelines.

Agriculture and raw-material processing were still considered the developing world's comparative advantage at the end of the 1960s. Almost 90 percent of Third World exports derived from primary products. In 75 percent of countries, these exports were concentrated in three crops—a very dangerous situation. If their price fell, the farmer could cross the line from feast to famine. Certainly agriculture in the early postwar years deserved more public spending than it got, even discounting the Green Revolution. Farming, after all, is what most people did to survive. But the developmental state rejected static comparative advantage. Taiwan's policy toward agriculture was a powerful model: feed the goat as you milked it.

Raul Prebisch, the Argentine who headed the United Nations' regional office in Chile, was one of the fathers of import-substitution theory. As mentioned earlier, he argued in the 1950s that there was a systematic tendency for the prices of many primary products to fall relative to those of manufactures, which benefited from intellectual property rights and new technologies that replaced natural resources with synthetics. As incomes in developed countries rose, their demand for raw materials rose—but by less. The deterioration in the "terms of trade" of agricultural goods was immiserating. More raw material exports had to be given just to get the same amount of manufactured imports in exchange. For his heterodox attack on comparative advantage, Prebisch was branded a bogeyman by the American State Department, as recorded in a World Bank history. But Prebisch was right about the terms of trade and short-run commodity price fluctuations. Even at the end of the century, developing countries were suffering from terms-of-trade losses. The loss was about $5 billion a year from 1981 to 1985, almost $55 billion a year from 1989 to 1991, and $350 billion for the period 1980 to 1992. The terms-of-trade loss was a major factor in the rise of these commodity exporters' foreign debt, as they strove to maintain a minimum of essential imports.[4] The burden of commodity price recession fell disproportionately on sub-Saharan Africa, the region least able to make structural adjustments. This was the penalty of not succeeding in import substitution.

Escaping from life as a farmhand and entering school for a better job was a dream that drove the struggle for colonial independence. The hope of upward mobility inspired millions of youths to migrate from the countryside to the towns after World War II in search of housing with electricity and sanitation services, skilled employment, education, entertainment, and the arts. The imperial idea that natural resources would forever be the engine of growth—when they already accounted for nearly 90 percent of total exports—was wishful thinking, especially since life as an agricultural hand was so hard.

As an example, on the large tea-growing estates in Sri Lanka, owned by multinational firms like Twinings, women walked from the huts where they lived to report for work at 6 a.m. They were then assigned a field to pick which might be miles away. The work was strenuous and hot. By noon the temperature could reach 90°F and the pickers' head-baskets were heavy. The women took one-hour breaks, then worked until 5 or 6 p.m., and finally returned home to make dinner for a family. There was no water or electricity to help in the preparation because the lines of huts where they lived were built over 100 years ago by even poorer Sri Lankans for the British.

Whatever the theorists said, people voted with their feet. Throughout the Third World, urbanization went hand in hand with industrialization. Between 1950, 1970, and 1990, population (in millions), rose from less than one million in 1950, to 1.9 in 1970 and to 5.9 in 1990 in Bangkok; from 2.8, to 6.0, to 13.0 in Bombay; from 1.4, to 2.6, to 4.4 in Santiago, Chile; and from 1.4, to 5.4, to 10.6 in Seoul.

Chile was the country most successful in targeting agriculture, exporting tropical fruits and vegetables to the United States counterseasonally—when it was winter in the United States, it was summer in Chile. But Chile had a highly unequal income distribution due to the concentration of raw materials. The government, rather than the private sector, had had the foresight to make agro-industry a leading sector, investing heavily in agricultural projects in the 1960s. But the results are ambiguous. Chile started the postwar period with a per capita income roughly twice that of Taiwan (which has about the same size and arability as Chile) but ended the century with a per capita income *barely half* Taiwan's, which in the meantime had targeted manufacturing growth. Manufacturing was at the heart of modern economic growth because it had the power to create new skills. These skills could afford to be rewarded at rates that left agricultural wages in the dust.

VI The Joy of a Job

Much better as an engine of growth than exporting natural resources was exporting *low-end manufactures*. This was a real possibility in the 1960s that conformed with the law of comparative advantage. American garment manufacturers in the Northeast first moved their production to the non-unionized South and then to Asia. Japan was the first location for American outsourcing and investment in labor-intensive manufacturing. But when Japan's wages rose rapidly in the 1960s under its "growth-doubling" plan, foreign firms fled in search of lower wage rates in an equally good environment—first to Hong Kong, then Singapore, Korea, and Taiwan, then Malaysia, Indonesia, the Philippines (a favorite with Japanese foreign investors), and Thailand. As the electronics industry boomed, the Silk Road was transformed into the Silicon Road. Television assembly arrived in Taiwan around 1965 with TV manufacturers such as Philco, Admiral, RCA, Motorola, and Zenith, most out of business now. Japanese firms, led by

Matsushita, Sanyo, Sharp, and Toshiba, joint-ventured with Taiwanese companies. Then came producers of calculators, followed by computers and semiconductors, and soon manufacturers of cell phones.

Virtually none of these foreign firms "manufactured" in Third World locales; they simply assembled parts and components, some made locally, most imported. Later, electronics firms "outsourced" to local assemblers. Innovators of high-tech products located assembly work abroad when gross margins fell to a trigger level. Because unit profits are low, efficient assembly requires large volumes, speed to market, and, above all, cheap, reliable, uncomplaining labor.

Labor-intensive manufacturing had its critics, because labor-intensive exporting often went hand in hand with subsistence wages, unsafe working conditions, and dead-end jobs. Nevertheless, exporting labor-intensive manufactures had one enormous advantage: jobs—and everyone wanted one. Young women workers found new freedom away from their families when they lived in factory dormitories, as anthropologists studying export "processing zones" found in Korea and Taiwan. To reduce labor turnover, companies sometimes provided workers with high school enrollment. National savings rose, and foreign exchange became more abundant. Local managers in foreign plants got state-of-the-art experience. In Taiwan, foreign-owned firms were a rarity by the 1990s, especially in electronics, but most top managers had apprenticed with an American or Japanese TV company in the 1950s and 1960s.

Washington listened to America's big subcontractors, who re-exported to the United States products assembled abroad. They paid no tariffs on the share of an import that had an American-made component or part. Only the labor costs of foreign assembly got a tariff slapped on it. This policy indicates that U.S. markets were not really open for the labor-intensive products that the Third World could export. The incentive for market opening was to satisfy American business.

The problem with exporting manufactures was not that there was too much exploitation, but that there was not enough investment to go around. Because of intense competition for foreign capital that created jobs, only a handful of Third World countries benefited from low-end export-led growth. Asia surpassed all others, owing to contacts with Japan and relatively reliable trans-Pacific transportation. Asia also had good infrastructure and *extremely* low wages, given its high population density. Low wages made all the difference. For example, when American television industries first relocated overseas, producers like RCA assembled their sets in Mexico—but wages were too high there, and they headed for Taiwan.

Over time, more and more American, European, and Japanese enterprises chased cheap labor, and moved their labor-intensive operations overseas. But export-led growth lacked the punch it had when it was concentrated in only a few countries, in the heyday of the First American Empire. By the mid 1990s, production was spread over as many as 225 export-processing zones in Asia and 41 in Latin America. Owing to an excess of suppliers, exporting low-end manufactures ceased being dynamic, and soon no one could compete against China. Even Asia could only extract the juice from exports by actively creating import-substitution industries side-by-side.

VII A Law Leans Leeward

The developing world, especially countries with manufacturing experience, built a set of institutions malleable enough to modernize industry. The strategy they used to industrialize was import substitution. With careful planning, they began manufacturing at home many of the products they had formerly imported. This reduced pressure on their balance of payments and satisfied pent-up domestic demand for semi-necessities ranging from air conditioners to scooters and trucks.

Import substitution violates the law of comparative advantage, but sometimes even a great law needs revision. After World War II, the assumptions of comparative advantage no longer held, and this distorted the predictions of the theory. However the Royalists reviled it, the engineers made import substitution work. For the first time in history, modern industries arose in parts of the Third World under a powerful yet relatively permissive empire.

But how, in fact, were the Royalists' legitimate objections to import substitution overcome? How did the Third World's inward-looking industries become the export-oriented powerhouses that gave critics around the world—from the Netherlands to Nebraska—such strong competition?

6 The Light of the Moon

Auto assemblers in Brazil had to meet an extremely ambitious domestic-content schedule to be eligible for the full range of financial subsidies. Each year their vehicles had to contain an increased percentage of domestically purchased components.

By July 1, 1960, trucks and utility vehicles were to contain 90 percent domestic content, and jeeps and cars, 95 percent.

Helen Shapiro, *Engines of Growth*

I Rigging Prices

Government intervention in import substitution was pervasive, not least of all in terms of "getting the prices wrong"—rigging prices with subsidies to make hard-nosed entrepreneurs willing to enter new industries. If subsidies were less common in Asia than Latin America, it was just because Asian entrepreneurs enjoyed lower labor costs and had fewer investment alternatives. The World Bank, in its *East Asian Miracle* report (1993), confessed to a list of price-"distorting" policies in the fastest-growing region of the world:

> targeting and subsidizing credit to selected industries, keeping deposit rates low and maintaining ceilings on borrowing rates to increase profits and retained earnings, protecting domestic import substitutes, subsidizing declining industries, establishing and financially supporting government banks, making public investments in applied research, establishing firm- and industry-specific export targets, developing export marketing institutions, and sharing information widely between public and private sectors.[1]

Governments also bailed out infant industries in trouble (like Korea's shipyard) and set "local content" rules to help small- and medium-sized parts producers (such as in Brazil's automobile industry). Markets were regulated, especially financial markets. To reduce waste, licenses to enter new industries were controlled. In Taiwan, a large-scale firm couldn't expand without a government OK. What the World Bank's report omits is why the interventions worked.

Import substitution was designed to help Third World countries enter heavy "mid-technology" industries that required large capital investments (such as steel) and nontrivial technology (such as petrochemicals) to compete against the entrenched big businesses of advanced countries from Germany to Japan that for years had been earning monopoly rents (as in overhead cranes) and employing thousands of skilled workers (as in automobiles). But there were negative elements to heterodoxy. Import substitution involved "picking winners" (repressing market forces), "rent seeking" (corruption), inefficiency (overriding market prices), and failing to export (Third World heavy industries were supposedly overpriced and overweight). The largest source of complaint was the repression of exports.

Some of these problems were real, such as corruption, but some were imaginary: picking winners was not really an issue when role models and road maps abounded from advanced countries for industries far from the world's technological frontier.[2] But generally the Royalists implied that the developing world was either too weak, ignorant, or stupid to circumvent hard problems associated with picking profitable industries to develop.

In fact, the least developed countries suffered from a lack of manufacturing experience. Import substitution inched along but then disappeared as countries fell into debt. But the more experienced developing countries innovated their way around the holes, tacking performance standards onto subsidies. Soon their exports began shaking up the Royalists' domains.

II Alexandria's Library

Google it, research it, rummage around the great Alexandrian library for it, and you'll find that there is no obvious reference in history to a "development bank" before World War II. The invention of maverick minds from late-industrializing countries, development banks lent at below-market interest rates to finance "strategic" industries, *and then monitored their loans*. A country's criteria for lending, and its monitoring capabilities, say a lot about its rate of growth.

The criteria for Brazil's development banking emerged out of historical circumstances. According to the Banco Nacional de Desenvolvimento Econômico e Social (BNDES), the development bank: "The second administration of President Getulio Vargas, begun in 1950, inherited from the previous administration a nation anxious for change. The favorable balance of trade was being weakened by the importation of heavy industrial products and equipment, the rise in post-war consumption and international fuel prices. Given such a dilemma, the nationalistic middle class emphatically called for funds for development of basic industries." None of this precluded the goal of raising exports, often seen as a conflict with import substitution: "Between 1958 and 1967, fully one half of BNDES' funds went to steel making, transforming Brazil, at the first stage, into a self-sufficient steel producer and, later, into a major exporter of steel products." Moreover, the policies of the BNDES changed over time: "Beginning in 1974, with the oil crisis that suddenly hit Brazil's balance of payments hard, the government decided to intensify its import substitution program, as set out in the second National Development Plan." BNDES began to finance "principally two major sectors: capital goods and basic raw materials, consisting of minerals and ores, steel and non-ferrous metal products, chemical and petrochemical products, fertilizers, cement, pulpwood and paper."[3]

Taiwan's heavy industries were targeted as early as 1961 to 1964, during the Third Plan, when its Ministry of Economic Affairs issued a report arguing, "Heavy industry holds the key to industrialization as it produces capital goods. We must develop heavy industry so as to support the long-term steady growth of the economy."[4] At the same time, exportables such as watches and other electronic products were promoted. After most heavy industries were, in fact, developed (steel, shipbuilding, petrochemicals, machinery), and the second energy crisis occurred (1979), goals changed. In 1982, the Taiwan government began to promote "strategic industries" (machinery, automobile parts, electrical machinery, information, and electronics) based on six criteria: large linkage effects, high market potential, technology intensity, big value-added, low energy intensity, and friendly to the environment.

The selection of industries to be promoted in Thailand, as stated in the 1950s, also had multiple criteria. First, they had to save a lot of foreign exchange. Second, they had to have strong linkages to other industries. Third, they had to utilize domestic raw materials. Yet another reason for promotion, according to the Ministry of Industry, was to gain technological knowledge: "Hopefully, the industries to be promoted such as automobiles, chemicals, shipbuilding, and so forth will transfer technological knowledge from developed countries."[5]

India's development plans listed objectives that were broader and more political than those of other countries, which is maybe why it grew more slowly: (1) a faster expansion of basic industry than of light industry, small firms than large firms, and the public sector than the private sector; (2) protection and promotion of small industries; (3) reduction in disparities in regional location of industry; and (4) prevention of economic power accumulating in private hands.

According to Turkey's Second Five-Year Plan (1968–1972), it was important to promote manufacturing because it was the sector that would "pull" the economy ahead in the future. Industry priorities were chemicals, commercial fertilizers, iron, steel and metallurgy, paper, petroleum, cement, and vehicle tires. The plan stated: "Intensified investments in these sectors will create to a large extent import substitution effects and lay the necessary foundations for industrialization in the long-run."[6] At the same time, Turkey's plan set targets for a large increase in exports, and the textile industry was heavily promoted.

The principles that guided Mexico's development bank in the early 1960s were to assist those industrial enterprises whose production could improve the balance of payments, achieve a better industrial integration, induce savings, or increase the level of employment. By the late 1980s, after a debt crisis, the bank's annual reports favored new principles to "promote the restructuring, modernization and financial rehabilitation of companies as a way of achieving better efficiency and production, which is necessary in order to increase exports and substitute for imports permanently, thereby reaching a level of international competitiveness."[7]

According to the 1969 *Annual Report* of the Korea Development Bank, top priority in lending was given to export industries and industries designated in a Bank Act that "improved the industrial structure and balance of payments." These included "import substitute industries."[8] Import substitution and export promotion were not seen as antagonistic; both involved large, long-term capital investments. By 1979, the end of Korea's heavy industry drive, the following factors were emphasized in financial commitments: the economic benefits to the nation, the technical and financial feasibility of a project, its profitability, and the quality of an applicant's management.

Comparative advantage was missing as a criteria in development banking because it was unworkable. Only if an industry succeeded was it proved, after the fact, to hold a country's comparative advantage. But from the looks of it, the criteria development banks followed were reasonable enough. No country was overambitious in targeting high technology, and no country focused on small niches that were impossible to enter given the specialized know-how they required. All the criteria pointed to mid-tech, but herein lies the rub.

Mid-tech industries were fiercely defended by incumbents because this was their bread and butter. In the case of the machine tool industry, which Japan wrested away from the United States in the 1980s, Japanese machine tool companies spent heavily on R&D. They fully automated production and served every major market. Their high-end models became the eighth wonder of the world. But even the most innovative Japanese machine tool companies wouldn't abandon their mid-end lines because this is where they made their money. Entry into machine tools by new Korean and Taiwanese manufacturers was extremely tough.

Except for the largest late developers, China and India, the success of import substitution can be measured by exports. Could development banks bring out the exports, or, as the Royalists worried, was the domestic market the end of the line?

III The Great Mother

Whatever the stage of development, import substitution tended to occur *before exporting*. The Royalists separated import substitution and export-led growth analytically, as though they were bipolar opposites, one bad, one good, but the two were tightly intertwined insofar as one had to precede the other. Import substitution was the mother of exports.

Even in Japan, "unit costs were reduced by increased domestic demand and mass production before the export-production ratio in growing industries began to be boosted."[9] Similarly in Brazil, in the period 1960 to 1980, "exports resulted not only from further processing of natural resources, ... which ... enjoyed a comparative advantage, but also from manufactures that firms learned to produce during the import-substitution phase." In fact, "export performance after the 1960s would not have been possible without the industrialization effort which preceded it as export growth was largely based on sectors established through ISI in the 1950s." Later, "import substitution policies created the capacity to export; the dominant export sectors of the 1980s and 1990s were the auto industry and those intermediate and heavy industries targeted for import substitution in the wake of the 1973 oil shock." In Mexico, the chemical, automobile, and metalworking industries were targeted for import substitution in the 1970s and began exporting 10 to 15 percent of their output in the 1980s: "Much of the rise in non-oil exports during 1983–88 came from some of the most protected industries."[10] The Chilean economy was able to adjust to an abrupt shock in 1973; "a portion of this response capacity, especially in the export sector, was based on the industrial development which had been achieved earlier through import-substitution policies."[11]

In Korea, "the shift to an export-oriented policy in the mid-1960s did not mean the discarding of import substitution. Indeed, the latter went on along with the export-led strategy. Export expansion and import substitution were not contradictory activities but complemented each other."[12] In electronics, "the initial ISI phase of the 1960s was critical to the development of the manufacturing skills that enabled [the chaebol] to become the efficient consumer electronics and components assemblers of the 1970s. Indeed, ISI in consumer electronics parts and components continued in the 1970s after domestic demand from export production justified it." By 1984, heavy industry had become Korea's new leading export sector, exceeding light industry in value, and virtually all of Korea's heavy industries had come out of import substitution, just as textiles had done in the 1950s and 1960s.[13]

In Taiwan, "in the first half of the 1960s, most of the exports came from the import substitution industries. Protection from foreign competition was NOT lifted. Getting subsidies to export was extra." In Taiwan's electronics industry, "there is no clear-cut distinction between an import substitution phase and an export promotion phase. Even though the export of electronics products speeded up since the early 1970s, the domestic market for electronics products was still heavily protected through high import tariffs. Whether protection was necessary for the development of local electronics firms is controversial. However, we do observe that the protection of consumer electronics products forced Japanese electronics firms to set up joint ventures with local entrepreneurs and to transfer technologies to local people which helped to expand their exporting capabilities."[14] In

Thailand in 1985, approximately 50 percent of exports (excluding processed foods) emerged out of import substitution. In the case of Turkey in the 1980s, "the growth in manufactured exports did not stem from the establishment of new export industries, but from existing capacity in industries that before had been producing mostly for the domestic market (that is, industries which had originally been established from import substitution)."[15]

A couple of decades later, China's leading firms were also first building their capabilities through import substitution, and only then venturing into export markets. TCL Company was formed in 1981 with a $5,000 loan from a local government in Guangdong province, and became a leading Chinese brand name in TVs, personal computers, air-conditioners, and cell phones (the balance-of-payments busters). According to its president, TCL aims to become a global household name, but first it has to succeed at home, where it faces local competitors battling for turf on the basis of low wages, and multinationals leveraging their reputations and know-how. TCL lacks proprietary technology, something it aims to rectify with the establishment of five research and development centres, including one in Guangdong with 700 researchers.[16]

Some exports did not come out of the import-substitution process directly, but were produced by *firms* that emerged out of it. The managerial and technological expertise of import-substituting firms in Asia gained them a business reputation and contracts with American firms searching for a lower wage locale than Japan to produce their parts and components. This sequence was also true of most of the Third World's diversified business groups, which were the model of big business after World War II in Asia, Latin America, and the Middle East, given their absence of proprietary technology. These groups typically first began serving the domestic market and then diversified into exporting.

Simply exporting proved to be too tough a first step for firms lacking original expertise or connections to markets in advanced countries. Apart from highly labor-intensive manufactures, *which needed no practice at home,* virtually all mid-tech industries first exploited their knowledge of their home market before venturing further afield. An exception to this rule was the Korean shipbuilding industry, which was designed to export from the start. But even here, the first few ships had to be sold at home, or the firm would go under.

Government economic intervention is always vulnerable to corruption, abuse, and inefficiency. Government failure may be as detrimental to development as market failure. Nevertheless, the presumption that all Third World governments simply threw subsidies to targeted industries without any controls on them turns out to have been fake. What lay behind successful postwar industrialization was a monitored system of controls on subsidies. Neither import substitution nor export-led growth was a free-for-all. In many cases, especially that of Korea and Taiwan, exporting was made a condition for domestic protection.

IV Nothing Is for Free

To minimize the inefficiencies of import substitution, countries built a complex set of institutions that amounted to a "control system." These systems attached performance standards to subsidies, including the tariffs, entry restrictions, and cheap credit that governments allocated to pioneering firms. Just as developed countries gave innovators patents by way of an incentive and reward, developing countries gave learners protection and other financial aids, but not for nearly as long as the duration of a patent, and not with nearly as little controversy. The guiding principle of the best bureaucracies—politics permitting—was to give nothing away for free. *Reciprocity was the ideal.* If the government gave a firm a financial incentive, the firm would have to give something back to the government in exchange, such as reaching a certain export target, output level, investment rate, or management practice. Reciprocity helped governments. If projects succeeded, they got more tax revenues and popular support, and most of all, they got more power. The elitist development banks, flagship of the "developmental state," subjected their clients to monitorable conditionalities.[17]

In the case of Brazil's preeminent development bank, BNDES, its contracts with borrowers stipulated clear and comprehensive performance obligations. A contract with a leading pulp and paper manufacturer in the 1970s, for example, stated that the company had to prove that it had hired a Brazilian engineering company to do the detailed design for an expansion; BNDES had to approve the company's general plans to establish an R&D department; and the company had to have its technology contracts registered with the appropriate government organization to insure that they were not overpaying for foreign technology. Another company had to hire two consultants (one Swedish, one Finnish), and these consultants had to approve the company's choice of technology. BNDES had to approve the company's contracts with the consultants.[18]

A contract for financial strengthening between BNDES and a leading capital goods manufacturer from 1983 to 1986 specified that in 60 days, the company had to present an administrative program for the reduction of operating costs. In 120 days it had to present a plan for divesting itself of one operating unit. Another capital goods supplier had to show BNDES a plan for relocation of certain production capacity, improvement of productivity, and strengthening of financial variables. As part of the reorganization program, the company had to hire a controller and implement an information system that was modern and that widened the company's scope of data processing. The company also had to modernize its cost system and improve its planning and control of production (within so many days). In a steel contract for expansion, the steel maker was required by BNDES to modernize its management system, including a revision of its marketing and distribution function for domestic and foreign sales. Its cost system had to be upgraded with a view toward reducing its number of personnel as well as its inventory, according to prespecified benchmarks.

BNDES also made clients reach a certain debt/equity ratio and liquidity ratio to insure financial soundness. The debt/equity ratio (amount of debt a company carried in relationship to the equity it held) was based on American banking standards, possibly because the United States had been an early lender to BNDES. Brazil's debt/equity ratio was low by East Asian standards—typically, debt could not exceed 60 percent of total assets. Hence, "large" Brazilian companies tended to be small by East Asian standards, whose debt/equity ratios were around 3:1 or even 4:1. Through its performance standards, BNDES could thus influence firm size. Bank clients were also prohibited from distributing their profits to stockholders of a controlling company. Companies were not allowed to make new investments of their own or change their fixed capital without BNDES approval. If a company required financial restructuring, it was forced by BNDES to divest itself of non-production-related assets.

In India, "Appraisal Notes" included conditionalities. For every loan, the Industrial Development Bank of India (IDBI) insisted on the right to nominate a director to a company's board. This practice was comparable to that of the big German banks, but the purpose of the IDBI was not to gain control of its clients' strategic decisions, but to gain information about them with a view toward exerting discipline over their operations. Other conditionalities in Appraisal Notes varied by loan. For example, in a loan to a large steel pipe manufacturer that represented 10 percent of IDBI's net worth, a condition of lending was that the firm form a Project Management Committee to the satisfaction of IDBI for the purpose of supervising and monitoring the progress of the project's implementation.[19]

In all countries, performance standards with respect to policy goals, as distinct from technical goals, were specified at the highest political level; bureaucrats only implemented them, but this gave them a lot of power. Export expansion was a major policy goal and performance standard.

South Korea, with the world's highest postwar growth rate of exports, induced firms to become export-oriented by making their subsidies—especially tariff protection of the domestic market—contingent on achieving export targets. In exchange for tariff protection, firms had to reach a certain export goal. This reciprocity was negotiated jointly by business and government and aired at high-level monthly meetings, as in Japan. These meetings were attended regularly by Korean President Park Chung Hee, and were designed to enable bureaucrats to learn and lessen the problems that prevented business from exporting more. Reciprocity also involved long-term policy lending by the Korea Development Bank (KDB). Starting in 1971, at the commencement of Korea's heavy industrialization drive, the KDB began to offer credit "to export enterprises recommended by the Ministry of Commerce and Industry." The more a company exported, the more likely it was to receive cheap, long-term loans. After 1975 the government made a lucrative license to form a "general trading company" contingent on big businesses reaching a certain level and diversity of exports. These qualifications unleashed fierce competition among Korea's big business groups at a time when the emergence of heavy industries was dampening competition at the industry level. If a targeted firm in Korea proved to be a poor performer, it ceased being subsidized—as evidenced by the high turnover among Korea's top ten companies between 1965 and 1985.[20]

The reciprocity principle in Korea operated in almost every industry. In electronics, for example, a publication from Japan's trade organization, JETRO, states, "the question could be asked why the chaebol [big company]-affiliated enterprises did not confine their business to the domestic market where they could make large profits without difficulty. The primary reason was that the government did not permit it. An important Korean industrial policy for electronics was protecting the domestic market. In return for protection of the domestic market, the government required the enterprises to export a part of their production."[21]

Taiwan, with the world's second highest growth rate of exports, also tied subsidies to exporting. Cotton textile, steel products, pulp and paper, rubber products, cement, and woolen textile industries all formed industry associations and agreements to restrict domestic competition and subsidize exports. Permission to sell in Taiwan's highly protected domestic market was made conditional on a certain share of production being sold overseas. In the "strategic Promotion Period" of Taiwan's automobile industry, from 1977 to 1984, the Ministry of Economic Affairs required new entrants into the industry to export at least 50 percent of their output (only parts producers succeeded, however).[22]

Other countries also connected subsidies with exporting, only in different ways and with different degrees of success. After the first energy crisis in 1973, Thailand's Board of Investment changed its policy toward the textile industry. Overnight it required textile firms (whether foreign, local, or joint venture) to export at least half their output to qualify for continued BOI support. To deal with labor "exports" of high-tech managers to run Japan's Thai subsidiaries, the Thai government allowed only short-term import contracts so that Japanese companies had to train Thai replacements.[23]

In Indonesia, "counterpurchase regulations" stipulated that foreign companies that were awarded government contracts, and that imported their intermediate inputs and capital goods, had to export Indonesian products to nontraditional markets of equal value to the imports they brought into Indonesia. In the case of timber, concessionaires were required to export processed wood rather than raw timber; in the mid 1980s, plywood accounted for about one-half of Indonesia's manufactured exports. Moreover, joint venture banks and branches of foreign banks were required to allocate at least 50 percent of their total loans, and 80 percent of their offshore funds, to export activity (a policy that the East Asian financial crisis of 1997 destroyed).[24]

Turkey tried to promote exports starting in the 1960s, making them a condition for capacity expansion by foreign firms. When a Turkish development bank, Sümerbank, and a German multinational, Mannesmann, undertook a joint venture, both the Turkish and German managing directors believed that the Turkish government was constantly willing to help the company in its operations. Nevertheless, one point irritated foreign investors: any capital increase required the consent of the Turkish government. It also became government policy to agree to a capital increase only by forcing companies to take on export commitments. The government held that, in general, any profit transfers abroad had to be covered by exchanges through exports. Since Turkish industry (steel pipes in the case of the Sümerbank-Mannesmann joint venture) could not yet compete at world market prices, export sales did not cover costs, and export quotas were regarded as an incentive to increase efficiency.[25]

In the late 1970s, Mexico's oil company, Pemex, guaranteed private petrochemical producers a ten-year price discount of 30 percent on their feed stock in exchange for their willingness to export at least 25 percent of their installed capacity and to maintain permanent employment (the debt crisis of 1981–82, however, led to the cancellation of this plan).[26] Then, the North American Free Trade Agreement and American investment stimulated a surge in exports to the United States, to the exclusion of almost any other country.

In Brazil, a program authorized duty-free imports in exchange for export commitments. The Brazilian government established the program in early 1970, after negotiations with the Ford Motor Company over its introduction of the Maverick model. This program, which allowed for increases in import content and tax exemptions against export performance commitments, was in tune with Brazil's export promotion policies since the late 1960s. For other industries, Brazil's export incentives included a standard package of duty drawbacks and other tax rebates. In addition, firms could negotiate their own customized incentive package in return for a specific commitment to export a certain proportion of their output. This reciprocal arrangement especially helped the transport equipment industry. By 1990, about 50 percent of Brazil's total exports were covered by reciprocal incentives.[27]

India made exporting a condition for subsidies and privileges of various sorts, but usually the terms of the agreement were unworkable. In the textile industry, for example, the government agreed in the 1960s to waive restrictions on firms' restructuring if they agreed to export 50 percent of their output—but few firms did so because they lacked the capital to restructure. In 1970, export obligations were introduced for various industries; industries or firms were required to export up to 10 percent of their output. But the Indian government couldn't enforce many export requirements, except possibly in industries that were already export-oriented, such as garments and software. For example, the right to import computers was dependent on software exports within a certain number of years after purchase.[28]

Performance standards were thus an antidote to abuse and inefficiency in government intervention. They hardly worked perfectly. But because the technological capabilities of developing countries were weak, governments conceived a new and unique system of controlled intervention to promote industrialization. The rapid skill formation and industrialization in a few countries that consequently occurred in the thirty years after World War II are a tribute to a generation of managers and bureaucrats who worked diligently, and with little disabling dishonesty, contrary to the gossip behind their reputations.

V Maverick Monitoring

As development banks imposed operating standards on their clients, they tightened their own monitoring skills and procedures. Monitoring was increasingly built into lending arrangements such that compliance at one stage was made a condition for further loan disbursement. Development banks undertook careful appraisals of prospective clients, examining their managerial and financial status, past performance, and the merits of their proposed project.

In 1970, the Korea Development Bank "strengthened review of loan proposals and thoroughly checked up on overdue loans to prevent capital from being tied up. Business analyses and managerial assistance to clients were conducted on a broader scale." In 1979 the KDB introduced a new procedure to tighten control over lending: "In order to ensure that loan funds are utilized according to their prescribed purpose, disbursements of loan proceeds are not made immediately upon commitment. Instead, loan funds are transferred into a Credit Control Account in the name of the borrower and the money may be withdrawn only for actual expenditures. The Bank is therefore able to monitor closely the progress of each project."[29]

Thailand's Board of Investment appraised and monitored clients thoroughly, and if a company failed to meet BOI terms (stipulated in a promotion certificate), its certificate was withdrawn. Between January and December 1988, 748 firms received certificates for new projects, of which 37 certificates were withdrawn.[30]

Where the capabilities of borrowers—*and lenders*—were poor, the quality of development banking also suffered. Malaysia's development banks were designed to lend to local Malays in order to raise their relatively backward economic position vis-à-vis Malaysian Chinese entrepreneurs, but the banks' operations were hampered by "the poor performance of many debtors." A failure rate on loans of about 30 percent was reported because of a shortage of viable projects. But even the best projects did not properly prepare their business proposals. Hence, Malaysia's Bank Industri "has a thorough research team on which it relies heavily. It has adopted a target market approach, and the research staff plays the key role in identifying and evaluating new areas of the economy for the bank to penetrate. The researchers undertake very detailed industry studies, looking at all aspects of a potential project in order to gain familiarity with its strengths and weaknesses." Once a project has been approved, Bank Industri "insists on being an active partner. It stays jointly involved in the financial management with its partner, often operating joint bank accounts with its clients, which requires the bank to countersign all checks for payment of expenses."[31]

Generally, development banks were successful in creating a managerial culture in their clients because they themselves were managerial, often representing the most elite bureaucracy of the early postwar period. In the case of Mexico's development bank, NAFINSA, its "*técnicos* became a respected voice in government affairs. . . . Its influence has been diffused throughout the Mexican economy. Since its founding in 1934, the institution has been the training ground for numbers of bright and active men [*sic*] whose technical and political expertise has moved them into important government positions." (Unfortunately, data on NAFINSA were destroyed in an earthquake.) And Brazil's BNDES has been described as having "a strong sense of institutional mission, a respected 'administrative ideology' and a cohesive *esprit de corps*." According to two executives of Dow Chemicals Latin America, interviewed three years before the Pinochet military coup, the National Development Corporation in Chile excelled due to its "organization and thoroughness of planning, ... which sets Chile apart from some of the other countries that have engaged in similar activities. ... The management of key Chilean Government agencies ... are outstanding professionals who do not automatically change with each succeeding political regime."[32]

VI Free Thinkers Fall

The combination of import substitution and export-led growth effected a phenomenal change in the nature of economic development. As the either/or of export-led growth and import substitution vanished, there arose a group of developing countries with knowledge that combined both. Their growth was impressive; their trade was earth-shaking; their wage increases were worth examining; and their skill formation was striking. But reality changed faster than theory. When a debt crisis descended, the past was discredited and conveniently forgotten by a new American Empire.

The mid-income developing countries, many in the Middle East, were the real losers. They started acquiring manufacturing experience only *after* World War II. Countries like Algeria and Egypt were finally ready for advanced import substitution and exporting when the patron of postwar development fell.

7 Dien Bien Phu: Knowledge Is Eternal

During the spring of 1954, the Vietminh surrounded the elite of French forces and cut it off from reinforcement by land. Crucial to Giap's plans were the 105-mm. American howitzers, of equal or larger bore than much of the French artillery, that the Chinese had captured from Chiang Kai-shek's forces and handed over to Giap. The guns had to be broken down into many parts, then carried through jungle paths and over newly built steep mountain trails on bicycles, by tens of thousands of foot soldiers and peasant porters. The French were ambushed and overcome by sheer force. With white flags flying, they surrendered at Dien Bien Phu.

George McT. Kahin, *Intervention: How America Became Involved in Vietnam*

I The Factory and Battlefront Share Ideas

Empires rise and fall by means of war. The First American Empire parachuted into power after World War II and perished from its own "immoderateness" in Vietnam. Washington stayed as strong as ever, but its earlier policies died, leading to a turning point in North-South relations. Never had any great power passed away at the hands of a Third World nation with primitive weapons, patchwork industries, and aid from China, another Third World country. President Lyndon Johnson disparaged Vietnam as a "nation in pyjamas," but it put him out of a job.

The Third World had devised a new method to build its industries and a new method to make war, and they were similar in Vietnam. The skills that were to emerge in Vietnam's factories were akin to those it perfected on the battlefield. Both showed careful attention to minutia, like the Japanese battlefronts and factories before them.

Knowledge and OPEC (the Organization of Petroleum Exporting Countries) were also closely intertwined. However politically disjointed, OPEC was well informed about energy. Tarring OPEC for collusion, the Royalists missed the point. OPEC achieved its major goal of sustaining higher oil incomes by sharing information among members and organizing joint opposition to the "Seven Sisters," the biggest private oil companies. A study of the oil industry in the 1960s noted: "Above all, OPEC has always sought to justify its existence through its own competence and expertise."[1] Lord Balogh, adviser to British Prime Minister Harold Wilson, stated, "the Arabs have experts who have forgotten more than the Foreign Office ever knew."[2] The First American Empire declined because Third World leaders, with one foot in traditional society and one foot in Harvard, Oxford, and the Sorbonne, knew more about the workings of the postwar world than the United States knew about the ways of the Third World, whether Vietnam or OPEC. Knowledge won the day, and brought to the fore a new generation of savvy nationalists.

If the Second American Empire wants to survive, it must beware of more OPECs and Vietnams!

II Twenty Cents a Day

As late as 1944, Franklin Roosevelt remarked on Indochina (present-day Vietnam, Laos, and Cambodia), "France has had the country—thirty million inhabitants—for nearly one hundred years, and the people are worse off than when they were at the beginning. . . . The people of Indochina are entitled to something better than that."[3] According to a Vietnam newspaper from the 1930s, "Each male worker gets a little more than 20 or 30 cents a day and a woman or girl worker gets only 18 cents. Even so, when the time comes for us to receive our pay we seldom get the full amount. . . . The larger parts of our wages are taken by the supervisors and foremen . . . [and] our salaries are already too low. How can we survive with all these fines and cuts? We have become hungrier and hungrier."[4]

For Ho Chi Minh, leader of the Viet Minh, North Vietnam's nationalist movement, the years 1945 and 1946 were a disappointment similar to the one he had experienced after World War I. When Woodrow Wilson announced his Fourteen Points, the 28-year-old Ho took the man and his principles seriously. Ho splurged, spending his meager wages earned painting fake Chinese antiques in Paris, and rented formal attire to present himself at the Paris Peace Conference, something of a ridiculous figure in a white tie and tails. He brought with him a petition he had drawn up listing Vietnam's grievances against the French colonial regime, in the style of

Woodrow Wilson's Fourteen Points, asking for autonomy, not independence. But no one from the American delegation or any other delegation would receive him: "Ho discovered that Wilson's self-determination applied only to the Czechs and Poles and other white peoples of Eastern Europe who had been under German and Austro-Hungarian domination, not to the brown and yellow peoples of Asia or to the blacks of Africa."[5]

When Japan surrendered, Ho wrote to Truman that France had lost any moral or legal claim to sovereignty over Vietnam, Laos, and Cambodia because the French fascist Vichy government had sold Indochina to the Japanese. Japan ultimately ousted the French altogether as direct rulers in 1945. By contrast, Ho wrote, the Viet Minh had "fought ruthlessly" against Japanese fascism. Ho again received no response, either from Harry Truman, Clement Atlee, Chiang Kai-shek, or Joseph Stalin.

By 1946, the French had retaken North Vietnam. Ho had offered Vietnam to Washington as a "fertile field for American capital and enterprise," even hinting that he would give them a naval base at Cam Ranh Bay, one of the world's best deep-water harbors, if only the United States would protect the Vietnamese from the French. Then, during a petty dispute between the French and Vietnamese over control of customs at Haiphong Harbor, Hanoi's seaport, 20 French soldiers were killed. The French used the incident to teach the Vietnamese a lesson. Using American-supplied planes, ammunition, and uniforms, French forces bombed Hanoi for a day. An estimated six thousand Vietnamese civilians were killed. Less than four weeks later, the French issued a proclamation demanding that the Viet Minh dissolve its paramilitary and police forces and let the French assume control of Hanoi. This left Ho Chi Minh the choice of either resistance or capitulation. His resistance was soon denounced in the West as "communist aggression." Based on these incidents, Ho concluded: "We apparently stand quite alone; we shall have to depend on ourselves."

After Roosevelt's death on April 12, 1945, there was a power vacuum. The Japanese were defeated and the French were still interned. No one knew for sure who would govern Vietnam, but the fear of Russian aggression in far-off Europe determined the course of events. Truman told Georges Bidault, de Gaulle's foreign minister, that the United States had never questioned "even by implication, French sovereignty over Indochina," because the area might otherwise fall into the communist camp and weaken the French struggle against its own communist movement and "progressive elements."

The French military was too decrepit to retake Vietnam itself. Not only had it been beaten by the Germans, but it was now engaged in a conflict with another Third World country, Algeria. Truman asked Britain's military, mostly Nepali Gurkhas under British officers, to help in Indochina. Although Britain was now ruled by the Labour Party, its imperial policy remained unchanged. American officers in the China-Burma-India theater joked that the initials of Vice Admiral Lord Louis Mountbatten's Southeast Asia Command (SEAC) stood for "Save England's Asian Colonies."

The French, with American help, and the Vietnamese, with Chinese weapons, fought on and off for roughly seven years. Then in 1954, to the world's astonishment, France—a great power and ingrained imperialist, enjoying advanced technology, innovative entrepreneurship, and sublime culture—was roundly defeated by the Viet Minh in the battle of Dien Bien Phu. The French had dug themselves into a valley in a mountainous region in northern Vietnam near the Laotian border because they knew that the Vietnamese had no heavy artillery: "But the Viet Minh had organized a civilian transport force of a quarter of a million people, most of them landless peasants, who had carried Chinese heavy artillery, broken down into many pieces, on their backs along paths through the jungle and over the mountain." Overcome, the French surrendered.[6]

The Vietnamese army was headed by the military hero Vo Nguyen Giap, the son of a mandarin and a communist. In 1939 the French arrested his wife, daughter, father, sisters, brother-in-law, and sister-in-law, and killed them all in jail between 1941 and 1943. Giap avoided capture and became the head of resistance against both France and the United States. In his own words:

> In waging the Resistance War, we relied on the countryside to build our bases to launch guerrilla warfare in order to encircle the enemy in the towns and eventually arrive at liberating the towns.... In 1952–1953, our Party decided to mobilize the masses for a drastic reduction of land rent and to carry out land reform, implementing the slogan "land to the tiller." Hence, the resistance spirit of the peasants was strongly roused... and the National United Front was made firmer, the administration and army consolidated and resistance activities intensified....
>
> The enemy's strategic principle was to attack swiftly and win swiftly... given the enemy's limited forces.... Our Party set out the principle of a long-term resistance.... Time was needed to mobilize, organize and foster the forces of Resistance, to wear out the enemy forces, gradually reverse the balance of forces, turning our weaknesses into strength....

> To organize an army, the question of equipment must be solved. . . . The great part of our regular army and guerrilla units were armed with weapons captured on the battlefronts. . . . On the other hand, our Party guided the workers in the spirit of self-reliance, and found means to manufacture a part of the arms and munitions for the army. . . . They overcame very great material and technical difficulties in order to turn scrap-iron into weapons for our troops to exterminate the enemy. . . .
>
> These are a few of the problems of tactics we solved in the Dien Bien Phu campaign. They were solved on the basis of our analysis of the enemy's strong and weak points, combining technique with heroism and hard-working and fighting-spirit of a People's Army.[7]

Victory by the People's Army did not mean complete control of Vietnam, especially in the South. A Geneva Peace Agreement, signed in 1954, divided Vietnam temporarily at the 17th parallel (Vietnam remained separated between communist North and insurgent South until war ended). It also called for popular elections two years later. President Eisenhower wrote in his memoir, *Mandate for Change* (1963), "I have never talked or corresponded with a person knowledgeable in Indochinese affairs who did not agree that had elections been held at the time of fighting, possibly 80 per cent of the population would have voted for the Communist Ho Chi Minh as their leader."[8] Eisenhower's Army Chief of Staff, General Matthew Ridgway, persuaded him that intervention in Vietnam was futile because of its geography and politics, and would be fatal for American troops.

But nonintervention was not to be. Subversion in Vietnam was escalated by Edward Lansdale, the CIA agent who had successfully led anticommunist operations in the Philippines and was the model for Graham Greene's novel *The Quiet American*. The United States soon backed Ngo Dinh Diem, a mandarin and devout Catholic, a friend of Cardinal Francis Spellman and Senator John F. Kennedy, to beat Ho Chi Minh. The Americanization of the Vietnam War had begun in earnest, until the war ended in 1975, and with it, the First American Empire.

III The Culture of Learning

Vietnam's "People's Party" won the war against infinitely more powerful opponents because it had popular support and outstanding organizational capabilities. It was not only nationalist, winning direct political independence, but also anti-imperialist, weaning itself from French, American, and later Chinese indirect influence and control. Its organizational skills were premised on popular support, labor abundance, and precision planning from the top down and bottom up. These skills were similar to those later used to build new industries under peacetime conditions by all successful late developers. The "minute detail" by which the Tet offensive of 1968 was planned by Vietnam's National Liberation Front (NLF), with "soldiers rehearsing their tactics in life-size models," was analogous to how South Korea built its first steel mill in 1973: "Before operations commenced, steel workers rehearsed their jobs in an open field, shouting orders to one another."[9] The NLF's synchronous invasions of South Vietnamese cities under American control resembled the "just-in-time" inventory management system developed by Japan's Toyota Automobile Company, the first major postwar innovation of a non-Western company, achieved around the same time as the Tet offensive. The careful decentralization of power from the People's Party to grassroots organizations, all sharing information and responsibility, resembled the diversified business group that appeared in almost every latecomer, starting with the *zaibatsu* in Japan, in which scarcity of managerial talent was overcome by pushing authority down to the industry and then shop-floor levels, where knowledge of production was greatest. In countries with scarce capital and backward technology, whether Vietnam or Iraq, organization and coordination using abundant labor are key to success. But in Vietnam, the United States lost touch with labor. The people who meant the most were the Europeans. "Because of France's position as the keystone of U.S. European policies, American priorities in Europe—not Asia—brought U.S. power . . . to bear in Vietnam. Insofar as communism was then an issue, it was primarily its potential in *France* that shaped American Vietnamese policy."[10]

America's greatest victory was defeating communist insurgents in the Philippines, a former American colony. After Japan's invasion during World War II, the Peoples' Army Against the Japanese (or Hukbalahap) was formed. The communist Huks "were as determined enemies of exploitative landlords as they were of the Japanese." Nevertheless, they were defeated in a largely Catholic country by American agents under the CIA's Colonel Lansdale. America triumphed against the Huks because Filipino identity was "bolstered as much by the American colonial educational system as by conflict with Americans, perhaps a cause for the docility that characterized Filipino nationalism in the early years of independence, at least in comparison with nationalism in most of postcolonial Southeast Asia."[11]

But America's use of the Philippines as a model for Vietnam (and Cuba) was a mistake. The United States knew the Philippine terrain well but knew nothing about Vietnam: "Many serious students of Vietnamese history have realized over the years that the total disregard of the realities of Vietnam had doomed the American intervention from the start." Nationalism differed in the two countries: it was weak in the Philippines but intense in Vietnam after 1,000 years of Chinese occupation, nearly 100 years of French colonialism, and approximately 20 years of American warfare. As one (of many) "hardened" American reporters in Vietnam observed: "I finally realized we'd never win this war when I noticed that all of the streets in Saigon were named after Vietnamese heroes who fought against foreign invaders." The puppet governments were also different. Ramon Magsaysay in the Philippines gained the nomination of the opposition Nationalist Party, supported by the United States: Maysaysay's "warm handshake and willingness to campaign in the villages—with an American helicopter—plus his well-earned reputation for honesty and effectiveness in the Department of National Defense" won him a landslide victory in 1953. By contrast, Vietnamese President Ngo Dinh Diem violated the terms of a Geneva Agreement and never held a popular election. He was known for corruption and incompetence, increasing taxes without visible deliverables. The United States finally got rid of him in a coup in 1963 that involved Ngo's own generals and the American ambassador, Henry Cabot Lodge. Ngo and his brother sought asylum in a church, but were caught, thrown in a van, and killed by a junior officer, making it improbable that any other top Vietnamese official would ever trust and cooperate completely with the United States. "There was a national revolution going on, and the United States was not part of it."[12]

With misinformation, wild antiwar protests at home, and raging inflation, the First American Empire exited the stage.

IV Oil on Troubled Waters

During World War II, President Roosevelt approved Lend-Lease aid to Saudi Arabia to consolidate Ibn Saud's position over other tribes and insure supplies for the oil-hungry Allies. Because of Soviet proximity to nearly all Middle Eastern oil-producing countries, oil became an issue for American national security. In September 1944, the Arab League tried to exchange information and coordinate policy among oil-producing countries in order to maximize their incomes. This attempt was a predecessor to OPEC, formed in September 1960 at the urging of Juan Pablo Pérez Alfonso, Venezuela's minister of mines and hydrocarbons, who aimed to improve the harsh conditions imposed on oil producers by the major international oil companies and their security-conscious governments.

The Marshall Plan hastened Western Europe's conversion to oil from coal, the energy source of the first Industrial Revolution. By 1947, the United States had become a net oil importer. To reduce insecurity, the Organization for Economic Cooperation and Development, a Paris-based club of rich nations, wanted to locate refineries and petrochemical complexes near consumers, not producers. This would sever the oil supply chain and reduce the developmental linkages of crude oil production for poor yet petroleum-abundant countries. To empower themselves further, the oil companies merged with each other, creating giants such as Aramco, established by Arabian-American Oil, Exxon, and Mobil (which subsequently merged). Mergers increased their monopoly power and savvy to control complicated, nontransparent pricing arrangements.

The no-nonsense attitude of the big oil companies was evident by the 1930s, before oil and the Middle East became synonymous (Saudi Arabia's rich reserves were discovered only in 1938). In 1914, Shell began producing crude oil in Mexico. Mexico's hostility toward foreign oil companies started in the early 1920s when it demanded a higher share of profits and better conditions for oil workers. The oil companies refused. In March 1938, foreign oil holdings were nationalized. Great Britain broke relations with Mexico and, together with the United States, started to put pressure on the Mexican government for compensation. Other oil companies cooperated with Shell and boycotted Mexican crude in world markets. Mexican production almost ceased, and Mexico only became an oil exporter in 1975. During those long 40 years, Mexico developed its own national oil company, Pemex, which became capable of producing, refining, and distributing oil. With oil money and petrodollars in its pockets (the dollars of oil producers that were recycled in the 1970s by New York banks and then lent again to developing countries), Mexico invested in the development projects it had dreamed of since 1938. No sooner had its industries flourished than it found itself in a debt trap as oil demand collapsed around 1980.[13]

The punishment for nationalization was even harsher in Iran in the early 1950s. In the first two decades of the twentieth century, the British bought oil concessions in Iran at a price comparable to the 24 dollars that the Dutch paid the Indians for Manhattan Island. In 1948, amidst rising nationalism, delegates from Saudi Arabia and Iran went to Venezuela to study its new 50:50 profit-sharing plan with some of the Seven Sisters, a plan that was adopted in Saudi Arabia in 1950. The British-owned Anglo-Iranian Oil Company refused to grant a comparable demand from Iran's popularly elected parliament, the Majlis, headed by Dr. Mohammed Mossadegh. Iran's economy was sinking, but the United States withheld a promised loan, and the World Bank, whose president is always American, also reneged on co-lending. After nationalization, all American oil companies refused to purchase and market Iranian oil. The American majors were being prosecuted on criminal charges of collusion by the United States Justice Department, but these charges were dropped in the higher interests of national security. By 1953, the British Navy had established a blockade in the Arabian Gulf to stop shipments of Iranian oil to willing buyers. Shah Mohammad Reza Pahlavi of Iran, an American puppet akin to Ngo Dinh Diem in Vietnam, then tried to overthrow the popularly elected Mossadegh but failed. Three days later, the Shah retook the Peacock Throne with the help of the army, assisted by the American Central Intelligence Agency.[14]

The United States won twice from the coup: it got rid of the socialist Mossadegh, and it broke Britain's monopoly over Iran's oil. The Anglo-Iranian Oil Company was converted into a consortium in which American majors got a large share. Soon Iran's demand for 50:50 profit sharing was granted. But as in Mexico, one national security crisis created another. The Shah was popularly deposed in 1978 and replaced by a Shiite Islamic government, which the United States hated even more than they'd hated Mossadegh, precipitating a second energy crisis.

The hard-nosed business of oil prior to OPEC was again evident only two years after Mossadegh's overthrow. In 1956, the Suez Canal was seized by Egypt's President Nasser, who had dethroned the profligate King Farouk. Nasser wanted to build the Aswan Dam in order to provide electricity to the cities, countryside, and industry, and to extend Egypt's arable land beyond the Nile basin. For finance, Nasser had lined up a loan involving the United States, the World Bank, and the United Kingdom. But in the spirit of nonalignment, Nasser asked Britain to remove its air base from Egypt. The United States then declined the loan, arguing that Egypt wouldn't be able to repay it (Egypt had just purchased $300 million worth of arms from Czechoslovakia). When the United States withdrew, the United Kingdom and the World Bank also withdrew, although in theory the Bank was an independent, multilateral lending organization. Two days later, on July 21, 1956, Nasser nationalized the Suez Canal—or, more precisely, the assets of the private company that owned the canal, a French and British joint venture.

The technology transfer policies of this company were abysmal. It had convinced the world that the canal was difficult to run, so *no Egyptian had ever held any position of responsibility*. Yet, as R. L. Tignor writes, "In reality, the Suez Canal was a relatively easy waterway to operate."[15] The directors viewed the company as a provider of financial services, so profits were repatriated overseas, not reinvested in Egypt. At a time when the Egyptian military was radical, the Canal Company's directors were "intensely conservative in their political beliefs and actions, many of them having supported the fascist French Vichy government during the war." After nearly 100 years, Egypt had gotten almost no developmental benefits from one of the world's most strategic waterways, located on its own soil.

France, Britain, and Israel invaded Egypt; the United States remained neutral; and the predictable ensued. Using tankers, the United States and Latin America organized an oil lift to Europe by way of the Cape of Good Hope. The Suez Canal never regained its prominence, and Egypt never enjoyed the revenues that had once enriched the Anglo-French Canal Company. To finance the Aswan Dam, Nasser tightened his relations with Russia.

Thus, OPEC was formed against a background of intense Arab nationalism and international conflict, much like the Vietnam War after the battle of Dien Bien Phu. Oil was more important than ever, although prices were down and new distribution channels were being built. All things considered, the First American Empire's presence in the Middle East had become more, not less, precarious.

The OPEC body with the highest authority was the "Conference," which comprised all the oil ministers from member countries. The country with the greatest oil reserves—Saudi Arabia—had the greatest power. At first, Saudi Arabia was represented by Abdullah Tariki, a radical with visions of nationalization, but he was fired by King Faisal. To take his place, Faisal appointed a conservative, pro-American sheik, Zaki Yamani, whose moderating influence on OPEC lasted for roughly twenty years. Yamani was a capable and knowledgeable technocrat, having gained experience in his own oil-consulting firm after studying law at Cairo University, New York University, and finally Harvard Law School. A flamboyant Westernized Arab with eight children and three wives, Yamani arrived at OPEC meetings in a Rolls Royce and wearing expensive suits, shopping for jewelry when meetings were adjourned—hardly a Ho Chi Minh or Vo Nguyen Giap.

OPEC devoted the 1960s to gaining an understanding of the complicated pricing system of the oil companies. Although it never acquired control over its members' production quotas or international prices, which fluctuated with market demand and war, it worked diligently at discovering how members could increase their oil incomes. Their incomes were tied to tax rates and the basis for calculating taxation, royalties and the basis for expensing them, marketing allowances, discounts, and participation in foreign ownership, including nationalization.

The 1970s were a hotbed of Third World nationalism, and OPEC's incomes rose as never before. By 1980, the governments of Iran, Iraq, Qatar, and Venezuela owned 100 percent of their countries' major foreign oil producers, while Kuwait and Algeria held 100 percent ownership in nationally owned companies that had supplanted foreign producers. Saudi Arabia owned 100 percent of Aramco, and Libya owned 100 percent of Arabian Gulf. Nigeria owned 80 percent of Shell and 60 percent of Agip, Elf, Gulf, Mobil, and Texaco. The poorer the country in terms of oil supply, generally the lower the rate of participation. For example, Gabon's participation in both Elf and Shell was only 25 percent.

The 1970s' nationalist outbursts led to huge price jumps at the gas pumps in every American town. A coup by Colonel Muammar Qaddafi in 1969 convulsed Libya, which then led OPEC to play small independent oil producers off against the giants. The Yom Kippur War of 1973 led to a 70 percent increase in oil prices; eventually, oil prices quadrupled. The fall of the shah of Iran in 1978 and the occupation of the American embassy in Teheran led to a second round of oil price increases. World power shifted from the skyscrapers of the Manhattan corporate headquarters of the big oil barons, to the skyscrapers of the Viennese headquarters of OPEC, to the oil-producing countries. Global income was redistributed along similar lines. OPEC had set up a fund to help non-oil-producing countries in the Third World, but mostly they were left severely bleeding. Even Brazil, a country with modest oil production, saw its current account deficit rise from $1.7 billion in 1973 to $7.1 billion only two years later. The economies of most developing countries, except those of OPEC, became too weak to withstand an imminent debt crisis.

V Bone Crunching

After the Vietnam War and the creation of OPEC, it was all over for the First American Empire and also for most other Third World countries that had learned to think for themselves and talk back. During the early Reagan years, James A. Baker III, who came to the Treasury from the White House, devised new policies: "In return for less bone-crushing conditions imposed by the IMF and more money, debtor countries would have to reform their economies away from the *counterproductive* state-run systems."[16] A new era, of reform without growth, had begun.

8 To Hell in a Straw Basket

The Fed's tight money caused the debt problem. World exports doubled in the decade before that. The GNP of many developing countries doubled in ten years. Nothing like that has ever happened in the history of the world.

Walter Wriston (CEO, Citicorp), quoted in W. R. Neikirk, *Volcker: Portrait of the Money Man*

I The Importance of Being Rich

As inflation in the United States worsened because of OPEC policies and the Vietnam War, the Federal Reserve cut the money supply and raised interest rates. As a result, Third World economies that once delighted in new investment possibilities became destitute overnight.

Still inexperienced, developing countries under the First American Empire were accustomed to financial transactions being heavily regulated. Historically, the quarter-century after World War II was a period of extensive government surveillance. As B. Eichengreen argues in *Globalizing Capital*, "Interest rates were capped. The assets in which banks could invest were restricted. Governments regulated financial markets to channel credit toward strategic sectors." Capital controls were important because "they were part of the series of levees and locks with which the raging rapids were tamed."[1]

Banks, bigger and more vociferous than ever, petitioned the Treasury, and the Treasury pestered developing countries to free their financial markets. In 1984 and 1994, the Treasury published tomes that targeted specific institutions in specific countries that were derelict in removing controls. Although still naive, one developing country after another opened its capital markets for foreign business. Edward Bernstein, the U.S. chief economist at the Bretton Woods Conference in 1944 and Keynes's counterpart, a voice from another era, summed up the tragedy: "Commercial banks were raking in so much money that they didn't care about the danger of a debt crisis. The real surge in lending occurred after the 1979 oil-price increase. Where was the IMF? Where was the Federal Reserve Board? *It almost sounds as if we had inadequate supervision of what the banks were doing.*"[2]

When Mexico's liabilities to American banks reached $84 billion and default was nigh, the world's most sophisticated financial services industry was taken by surprise. According to a senior White House official, "Believe me, Mexico was the last thing on our mind."[3] As Richard Nixon had said about the developing world a few years earlier, "Nobody gave a damn." The Mexican financial collapse was contagious, and soon other indebted countries were on the verge of a financial crash. Then a lot of people cared.

Creditors can use two generic methods to collect their pound of flesh: They can help debtors grow fat and then skim off the cream, or they can make debtors become emaciated and then grab whatever they shed. Always, bankers have preferred the second method.

The advice of a British commission investigating Turkey's debt problem in the *1860s* was indistinguishable from the advice of the International Monetary Fund investigating Turkey's debt problem in the *1980s*: "Both programs recommend the government to reduce budget deficits, restrict monetary growth, and ensure real devaluation for short-term stability; and to deregulate markets, curtail the role of the state, and liberalize foreign trade and foreign capital inflows for long-term growth."[4] Nothing had changed despite all the new sophisticated tools of financial management and flow of knowledge from South to North.

Throughout this collapse, East Asian countries remained unaffected. Their debt crisis struck later, in 1997, which gave them 15 years of solid growth more than other developing regions. China, India, and Taiwan never fully deregulated their financial markets, *and never suffered a debt crisis*.

II Cigar Capitalism

Transparency and the U.S. Treasury are opposites that don't attract. A question and answer period to learn more about the Treasury might run as follows:

Outsider: What made Korea open its financial markets to the tune of $45 billion just before its financial crash in 1997?

Insider: Uh, don't know!!

Outsider: Well, if I really want to find out, I can. I can sue you under the Freedom of Information Act.

Insider: You do that. It will take about three years for you to get the documents, and then all the names you want to know will be blanked out for security reasons.

Financial markets are highly competitive because billions of dollars flow in and out each day. This means that financial transactions are transparent by definition. But the rules of the game are drawn and enforced by big players. When China's entry into the WTO was being negotiated in the 1990s, "a raft of Wall Street banks, investment banks, insurance companies and other financial institutions . . . pressured the U.S. Treasury to require China to loosen its capital controls and gradually permit the entry of foreign firms into China's domestic financial markets."[5] A lack of transparency plus big players are deadly for the poor and powerless.

The financial services sector operated according to reputation and trust—some call it cronyism. When the Third World debt crisis erupted, it was handled by the IMF and Federal Reserve. The managing director of the IMF was Jacques de Larosière, a close friend and fishing partner of Paul Volcker, the chairman of the Federal Reserve. Although this relationship made for good communication, outsiders didn't have a chance.

III Ignorance Is Not Bliss

The petrodollars generated by OPEC flooded financial markets in New York and London in the 1970s, pleasing both lenders and borrowers. Third World borrowers, public and private, saw an opportunity to invest in long-dreamed-of projects that were unprofitable at higher interest rates, such as amusement parks in Buenos Aires and automobile plants in Seoul. The enthusiasm of borrowers is comprehensible, but the zeal of lenders to part with their money is incomprehensible. Why would experienced bankers lend to poor countries that were likely to default?

Petrodollars were so cheap and relending was so profitable that banks earned high rates of return even if borrowers ultimately busted. Incentives in the private banking sector were also distorted toward *loan-pushing*. The bonuses of loan officers—part of a new global financial elite—often depended on how much they lent, so the incentive was to lend as much as possible and to get another job before a loan fell due. Most borrowing rates were variable, which is what pushed some countries over the edge. When interest rates rose in the American economy, interest rates rose on loans—see the small print.

Where, indeed, was the Federal Reserve Board? The U.S. consumer price index had reached 11 percent in 1978, a rate that was horrific to American pensioners and wage-earners. Americans were unused to banana-republic inflation. Luckily, the Fed was in capable hands, those of Paul Volcker, a consummate civil servant, having spent almost all his life in various government posts, including as Under-Secretary of the Treasury, with only a brief spell at Princeton and Chase Manhattan. At a dinner at Columbia University in 2003 honoring economic reporters chosen as Reuters Fellows, Volcker was asked which economist he respected the most. His answer was Keynes. Then he was asked why he hadn't warned the developing world of his plan to slash the money supply and rein in inflation. He said: "Because they wouldn't have listened."[6] Volcker's withholding of information from the Third World on a life- and death-policy, if only from absent-mindedness, symbolized the redistribution of knowledge from poor to rich countries. The world was rotating back on its axis.

Keynes once remarked that if you owe a bank $100 and can't repay, you are in trouble; but if you owe a bank $100 *million* and can't repay, the bank is in trouble. Wall Street was more vulnerable than other financial hubs because it had lent heavily to Mexico, and Mexico was the biggest developing country to verge on bankruptcy. The IMF and Federal Reserve joined forces and went into action—for a while laissez-faire was abandoned.

Mexico pleaded with the IMF and the Fed to let it grow fat and repay its loans with excess blubber, but the moneymen refused. The appeals of Mexican President José López Portillo, responsible for developing Mexico as a major oil exporter, fell flat. Volcker and de Larosière "stood firm against Mexico's efforts to try to keep its spending high and interest rates low and to impose exchange controls and keep wages high." Mexico's Yale-trained finance minister Jesús Silva Herzog even sided against his boss in favor of the moneymen! In López Portillo's teary farewell presidential address a few months later, he apologized to Mexico's poor for letting them down. Silva

Herzog, the former finance minister, became ambassador to the United States. Mexico borrowed more to avert bankruptcy. The strings attached required broad-ranging market liberalization. Mexico's developmental state was dismantled, and its growth rate began its decades-long decline.

According to Henry Kaufman, a big Wall Street bond trader, "Paul Volcker stands out as one of the great central bankers of the twentieth century." According to Walter Wriston, the CEO of Citicorp, Volcker wildly overreacted and killed the goose. (According to an interview with Volcker in the *New York Times*, Wriston saw himself as a rival of the Federal Reserve in terms of his influence on the banking system.)[7] Whatever the final verdict on Volcker, it is probably fair to say that the bailouts of the 1980s were astonishing for their lack of vision. They carried conditionalities similar to those under colonialism, despite an Asian alternative indicating where the world was going. Even the creditors in Ottoman Turkey did better! They were actively responsible for getting Basra's ancient silk industry up and running in order to generate more revenues for themselves, and they even imposed tariffs to keep domestic silk production going. Nothing as spunky as this activism occurred in the 1980s.

IV Raising the Dead

Washington put its money for recovery on privatizing the Third World's state-owned enterprises and enticing the entry of multinational firms. The debt crisis had devastated Third World companies. But if their ownership was transferred to foreigners, the fittest would survive (as would American industry). With enough foreign direct investment (FDI), it would be possible to raise the dead! In no event were Third World governments allowed into this new business.

From 1980 through 1995, foreign firms increased their share of total Brazilian output from 33 percent to 72 percent in the computer industry (one of the failures of import substitution), from 30 to 57 percent in the electrical machinery industry, from 41 to 64 percent in the nonelectrical machinery industry, and from 46 percent to 68 percent in the chemical industry.[8] Cross-border mergers and acquisitions in Latin America soared. Foreign acquisitions of companies rose, according to UN data, from $1.1 billion in 1988 to $63.9 billion in 1998.

Apart from Latin America's new elite financial managers, whose income depended on takeovers and privatizations, national governments and local companies began to have second thoughts about multinationals outside the labor-intensive industries of export-processing zones. Compared to the *best* nationally owned companies, the *average* multinationals left something to be desired because of their bureaucratic procedures and lack of entrepreneurial spirit. Maybe resources should be shifted to local firms for restructuring?

Bureaucratic control systems slowed the reaction time of foreign subsidiaries. In India's pharmaceutical industry, a local firm could be faster to market than the subsidiary of a multinational that had invented a drug in the first place. Samsung Electronics of Korea was starting to catch up with Sony Electronics of Japan in certain product segments. Embraer of Brazil was closing in on Bombardier of Canada. Tata Steel of India had already closed USX of the United States.

In colonial times, multinationals were rarely the first to invest locally in a new sector, the quintessence of entrepreneurship. They were not leaders, as shown in chapter 2. The experience of nineteenth-century America "strongly supports" this assessment,[9] as does the history of Japan: "When the Japanese had already demonstrated their general progressive drive and their specific industrial aptitudes, FDI in manufacturing made an appearance."[10] Even in India, foreigners were responsible for starting a few industries, including the railroads, but Indians took the lead in most of the rest.

As noted earlier, televisions were a big-ticket item in the late 1950s that advanced countries began assembling abroad, in their own factories, first in Japan and then in Mexico, Korea, Taiwan, and Singapore. CEOs of Taiwan's electronics companies say they learned modern management from American TV makers, but even here the foreign investor didn't really plough virgin territory. RCA was the first company in Taiwan's TV industry, but a Taiwan company, Tatung, already produced fans and rice cookers (with Japanese technology). Tatung's assembly lines were the teachers of thousands of Taiwanese workers, managers, and engineers. Its demand for parts and components jump-started Taiwan's dense network of small- and medium-sized enterprises, a must for most electronic products. The Taiwan government, recognizing that foreign manufacturers resettle in the country with the lowest wages, introduced incentives for joint ventures to be formed at home with Taiwanese and Japanese TV makers.

When electronic goods such as calculators, computers, and cell phones were outsourced, the multinationals no longer invested at all in their own production facilities abroad; instead, production facilities and detail design were in the hands of Third World companies. The multinationals sent them the basic architecture of a model and they did the rest. Outsourcing allowed the Third World's best firms to corner the market in manufacturing excellence and integration R&D. But indebted Third World enterprises were in desperate need of capital, and this made foreign direct investment look good. Foreign investment also looked good to a second generation of owners that was uninterested in keeping a family business alive.

Two problems plagued foreign direct investment. First, the countries that needed it the most (the poorest countries), received the least. Second, state-owned enterprises were supposed to be privatized to rid governments of lemons. But no one wanted to buy a lemon. Foreigners bought only the best companies that needed privatization the least.

Attracting foreign investment in the poorest countries was always an act of magic. Sir W. Arthur Lewis, who in 1957 wrote the development plan for Africa's first independent country, Ghana, triggered a lively debate over whether to welcome FDI. Finally, Lewis factored in a role for it. But no investment came, except to mine Ghana's raw materials. Just as most foreign investments in manufacturing went to (and came from) North America, Europe, and Japan, the share to developing countries was concentrated in Brazil, Malaysia, Mexico, Singapore, and eventually China.

Foreign investment can go a long way in a poor, small country. Between 1991 and 1996, FDI *as a percentage of gross fixed capital formation* was as high as 24 percent in Swaziland (a South African offshoot), 29 percent in Singapore (an active suitor of foreign investment), and 38 percent in Trinidad and Tobago (an oil-rich Caribbean island), all minuscule economies. Sometimes the share spiked in "hot" countries: oil-rich Nigeria (29 percent), touristy Guyana (35 percent), and opportunity-rich Vietnam (35 percent, where most investors were Asian).[11] Given Mexico's location, its comparative advantage was economic integration with North America. American investments in the *maquilas* in Mexico's export-processing zones boomed, but the rest of Mexico's economy was as slow as a graveyard. Even factories from the north began heading for China.

The average developing country was always being told to give itself away in marriage to a foreign direct investor even though such an investor had a small dowry. FDI accounted for a minuscule share of the South's capital formation outside the few examples named above. In the 1990s, the *average* annual share of FDI in capital formation was 4.4 percent in the world, 5.5 percent in the European Union, 6.5 percent in developing countries (including raw materials), 5.3 percent in Africa, 6.9 percent in South America, 1 percent in the Middle East, and 11 percent in China. In countries actively committed to growing their own national enterprises, the share of FDI was minuscule: 1 percent in India, less than 1 percent in Korea, about 2 percent in Taiwan, and below 4 percent in Thailand.

Under the Second American Empire, the natural-resource sector of poor developing countries was already owned and controlled by foreign companies, oftentimes very mean-spirited ones (Pechiney, the French giant multinational from colonial days, owns 51 percent in a holding company of alumina production in Guinea, which has the world's largest bauxite reserves, the second largest bauxite production in 2001, and the rank of only 159 out of 173 in the UN's human development index). Under foreign ownership of raw materials, profits were generally repatriated, and tax rates and royalties were a constant source of conflict with weak local governments. Exempting the era of the First American Empire, nothing much changed in the natural-resource sector from the colonial period to the Second American Empire. Because a large share of the wealth of the poorest countries was already under foreign control, and the poor didn't seem to be getting richer—if anything, they were becoming poorer—a development policy based on more foreign investment was blind.

Many poor countries nationalized their raw materials under the First American Empire and got away with it. They created state-owned enterprises that usually operated jointly with a foreign mining company. In most cases, corruption was kept to a minimum. Chile and El Salvador nationalized Anaconda Copper late, in the period from 1966 to 1976, but Chile kept mining under state ownership even during the neoliberal Pinochet dictatorship. Countries nationalized their raw materials to increase their tax receipts and royalties, which were important sources for financing their development, and for training local labor for managerial positions. Labor conditions at the time were primitive. Duncan Kennedy, a summer intern at Pechiney-Guinea in 1962 (and now a professor at Harvard Law School), interviewed African miners about promotion. Almost all claimed that most French supervisors were racist. When he reported a serious race relations problem to the chief operations officer, he was shown the door.

Under the Second American Empire, ownership went the other way: most state-owned mining enterprises were privatized. Canadian mining in Latin America exploded. Investors responded with policies of deregulation, privatization, state-downsizing, and export promotion encouraged by the International Monetary Fund and the World Bank.

Poor countries in the late 1980s, especially in Africa, needed the money from selloffs of their assets to balance their fiscal accounts. But ironically, privatization and tax incentives for foreign investors decreased government revenues from the mining sectors. Privatization was not only expensive but was also a one-shot deal.

In the early 1990s, the top 15 state-owned enterprises in the South were all in heavy industry. Out of 15, 13 were in petrochemicals or metallurgy, mostly iron and steel (see table 8.1). These were national champions with

Table 8.1
The Developing World's Top Fifteen Public Enterprises in Manufacturing, Ranked by Sales, Selected Countries

	Sales (mil US$)	Name	Country	Activities
1	21,023	Petroleo Brasileiro	Brazil	Petroleum
2	20,270	Petróleos Mexicanos	Mexico	Petroleum
3	11,836	Chinese Petroleum Corp.	Taiwan	Petroleum
4	9,900	Pohang Iron & Steel	Korea	Iron, steel
5	8,077	Indian Oil Corp.	India	Petroleum
6	6,833	Vale do Rio Doce	Brazil	Minerals, metals, paper
7	6,821	Petrobras Distribuidora	Brazil	Petroleum
8	5,924	Pertamina	Indonesia	Petroleum
9	4,021	Steel Authority Limited	India	Iron, steel
10	3,865	Taiwan Tobacco & Wine	Taiwan	Tobacco, spirits
11	3,207	Oil and Natural Gas Corp.	India	Petroleum
12	3,002	Hindustan Petroleum	India	Petroleum
13	2,490	Petronas*	Malaysia	Petroleum
14	2,126	Bharat Petroleum	India	Petroleum
15	1,201	Bharat Heavy Electricals	India	Diversified

*Sales figures are for 1990.
Sources: See citations and notes in Amsden (2001), p. 214.

few, if any, shades of corruption. They created de novo organizations, accumulated high levels of both managerial and technological capabilities, and diffused these capabilities to the private sector. Every state-owned petrochemical company spun out national chemical manufacturers downstream.

One way or another, the most powerful state-owned enterprises in savvy countries retained their national identity (except in Argentina). The most nationalistic, such as POSCO, Usiminas, and Vale do Rio Doce (Brazil's premier metallurgical company), were privatized such that no single owner emerged and the government retained a stake. Usiminas's voting shares were distributed among pension funds (26.8 percent); financial organizations (23 percent); Compania Vale do Rio Doce, which was itself sold to multiple owners (15 percent); Nippon Usiminas (13.8 percent), an original owner of Usiminas that was owned by Shin Nippon Steel; employees and employee pension funds (11.1 percent); and steel distributors (4.4 percent). Of 24 major Brazilian properties auctioned in 1991–1993, only 12 had a single major buyer. POSCO (Korea) was sold publicly to relatively small holders. To avert a hostile takeover, it arranged an equity deal with its old teacher, Shin Nippon of Japan. The inner core of Sunkyong, a major Korean business group, was Yukong Oil, a former public holding.

Unless a country has its own nationally owned firms, it can't "globalize" in the form of outward foreign investment. If only foreign firms exist in a developing country, the overseas investments of these firms can't redound to the developing country. Nationally owned firms continued to receive help from Third World innovation systems and the residual institutions that didn't die with the First American Empire. But in general, the Third World was starved for foreign capital to revive its own private enterprise—a victim of the North's fear of "excess" competition and the resurrection of the developmental state.

V Brains or Brawn?

The world changed when Paul Volcker's pen slashed the U.S. money supply without any warning to Third World creditors. The First American Empire received a second bullet through its heart, and this one hit the Third World as well. Countless developing countries fell into debt traps that kept them in the economic doldrums for decades. The medicine of privatization and foreign investment turned out to be weak tea.

Debt was the cost of deregulation of financial markets in countries without the institutions to support wild fluctuations in the supply and demand of capital. Inflows led to euphoria, but the ends didn't justify the means. Outflows led to euthanasia. Where is the accountability of those who assumed that wholesale deregulation of financial markets was *everywhere* right? Where was the transparency that the Treasury preaches?

It is best to think of accountability in terms of ideas rather than people. The Second American Empire's ideas were like a giant iceberg—dangerous because of their immutability and mostly out of sight.

As the slowdown in growth continued, the job of restructuring the Third World's debt-damaged business enterprises became more urgent. Companies had to be repaired and rationalized before they could be sold or saved. This job became harder and harder, given the Second American Empire's dislike of the developmental state.

9 America's Fatwas

The abrupt onset of intolerance for dissent contaminated the atmosphere for open intellectual inquiry on which good research depends.

D. Kapur et al., eds., *The World Bank: Its First Half Century*

I From Ideas to Ideology

When a company falls into debt, it falls behind its industry's norms. Its equipment grows obsolete, its machinery becomes dated, its product lines lose their sheen, and its R&D folds. Fixing requires new ideas and novel procedures, since foreign multinationals may not or cannot do the job. In developing countries with big business groups, such as Korea, one healthy group affiliate with retained earnings may help a sick sister. Or a company can always fire workers and restructure by saving wages. But this "pink slip" approach, popular in the United States, is usually not enough in the Third World, where wages are a tiny fraction of costs.

The Second American Empire used the fatwa to restructure. Decrees went out and there was very little the developing world could do about them. Nor were the ideas behind the fatwas novel. A Dark Age ensued, characterized as all such periods are by an absence of intellectual ferment and fresh knowledge. The ideas of the Second American Empire harked back to the great political economists—Smith, Ricardo, Malthus, and Marx. But what had once been original thinking became encrusted ideology—a hunch became a truth, and a theory lost validity due to invalid assumptions. Ideas that no longer held in changing times were bulldozed over to create the impossible: a "level field" on which experienced and unexperienced firms were supposed to compete.

Ronald Reagan's appointee to the World Bank during the debt crisis, A. W. Clausen (1981–1986), chose an ultraconservative economist, Anne Krueger, to head the Bank's Economics and Research Department. She purged 38 people on her staff, leaving in place only 7 "loyalists." The Bank's Personnel Department warned senior management that Krueger had adopted an "intelligence" system to detect her staff's divergences from politically correct views. The Bank's official history called this "thought control."[1] Because the United States counted for the largest number of votes on the Bank's board of directors (17 percent), its word was law. About 20 years later, Krueger was rewarded by President George W. Bush with the IMF's second-ranking position.

An informal "Washington Consensus" emerged that embraced the State Department, Treasury, Trade Representative's Office, NAFTA, World Bank, IMF, Inter-American Development Bank, Paris-based OECD, and Geneva-based WTO. All favored liberalization, deregulation, and privatization. Along with the developmental state, real debate became a thing of the past. Argument was reserved for details.

II Nowhere to Run

The World Bank was designed at Bretton Woods to be the electric power station behind Third World economic development. But it lived with a contradiction: it lauded the private sector, but *it never lent to it*. Lending to the Third World's private borrowers was left to the First World's private lenders; this was their business, and Congress would never support a public organization that infringed on private terrain. The World Bank at first financed infrastructure, then aid, forgetting about private Third World industry except for what was small in scale. The expectation was always that the Third World's industries would be restructured by multinational firms.

After the Clausen-era purges, the Bank's president became Barber Conable (1986–1991), an upstate New York Republican politician with almost no experience in economic development. Instead of asserting the Bank's independence, he was sympathetic to "strong pressures from the U.S. Treasury on the Bank to become more market and private sector oriented."[2] The Bank began making "structural adjustment loans" (SALs), which allowed an indebted country to pay for imports but not to pay for restructuring industries that competed with these imports. This was import substitution in reverse—promoting imports in lieu of domestic production. Soon more stringent conditions were attached to SALs. In the late 1980s, an average loan carried 56 conditions, ranging from the allowable size of a country's budget deficit to the acceptable mode of its pension funding.

A pioneer of Africa's SALs and a Clausen ally, Elliot Berg, maintained that Africa's development depended only on macroeconomic policies—not industrial policies, not technology policies, not immigration policies, but simply policies regulating the money supply and interest rate, period. Loans to Africa were "mainly intended to help bring Bank representatives to the borrower's policy-making high table," to familiarize them with macroeconomic principles, not to restructure.[3]

Developing countries lost almost all power over their own destinies as the Second American Empire tightened its policy screws. For example, "it would be fair to say that since 1988 Pakistan's economic policies, management, and performance, have been almost totally determined by the country's adherence to IMF/World Bank-sponsored structural adjustment programmes, and Pakistan's various governments have had no independent or original programme of their own."[4]

World Bank President James Wolfensohn, a Clinton appointee, used his "charisma, charm and frequently explosive temper to cajole and bully the bank's staff and board into changing the bank's focus toward a greater emphasis on alleviating poverty," rather than promoting loans for manufacturing investments.[5] Wolfensohn's muse was Amartya Sen, a philosopher and economics professor from Harvard and Oxford who had won a Nobel Prize. In *Development as Freedom*, Sen notes "two general attitudes to the process of development that can be found both in professional economic analysis and in public discussion and debates." One attitude "sees development as a 'fierce' process, with much 'blood, sweat, and tears'—a world in which wisdom demands toughness." Delicacies like democracy and civil rights are pushed aside. This approach represents raw capitalism at its worst, or the "dark Satanic mills" of Karl Marx. In contrast to hard-knocks capital accumulation, another view on development is promoted by NGOs, advocates of "small is beautiful," Professor Hernando de Soto and Professor Sen. This approach "sees development as essentially a 'friendly' process," one characterized by trade rather than production, "exemplified by mutually beneficial exchanges (of which Adam Smith spoke eloquently)," the social safety net, political liberties, or some combination of these "supportive activities."[6] Sen holds the same views as Pierre Joseph Proudhon, a French writer born impoverished in 1809, who opposed capitalism, communism, exploitation, and statism, and favored a self-managed society.

What neither Sen nor Wolfensohn seem to have remembered is that the two approaches must go together if development is to thrive, as they did in their native countries of India and Australia, respectively. Poverty alleviation will not succeed if capital formation fails, as discussed in chapter 4. Yet as East Asia increasingly threatened American industry, the World Bank pushed the tough approach to development aside.

The next president of the World Bank was a former close adviser of George W. Bush with hardly any banking experience: Paul Wolfowitz is rumored to have unsettled senior management by appointing a team of neoconservative loyalists to his inner circle. Neoconservatism went as far as supposing that even international emergencies requiring restructuring would be approached on a private basis. The greatest relief effort in modern history followed the tsunami in the Indian Ocean on December 26, 2004. Around 200,000 people were killed, thousands of children were orphaned, and more than half a million were left homeless. Private donations were unparalleled in their generosity to private charities such as Oxfam and Doctors Without Borders. But U.S. government support, from the military, was equally unprecedented. The helicopter carrier USS *Bonhomme Richard*, with a total of 24 heavy, medium, and light-lift helicopters, and the aircraft carrier USS *Abraham Lincoln* moved water purification systems, military rations, clothing, medicines, and medical equipment into remote areas. Six container ships that produced fresh water arrived on the scene. The UN emergency relief coordinator said that these military assets were "worth their weight in gold." This didn't stop a former USAID official and a senior fellow at the Hudson Institute, a conservative think tank, from expressing a popular opinion: "The fact is, foreign aid is being privatized."[7]

Intellectuals in the First American Empire—economists such as W. A. Lewis (Nobel Laureate in Economics from the West Indies), Raul Prebisch (head of the UN Economic Commission for Latin America), and S. Mahalanobis (India's chief planner)—were not altogether open-minded. Most were anticommunist as well as contemptuous of the Right. But one thing made them cosmopolitan: they inhabited a vast middle ground within which they tolerated a broad diversity of opinion, on issues ranging from tariffs to employment creation to development banking. Diversity was good for growth because it opened the mind. By contrast, intellectuals from the Second American Empire, numerous and diverse in gender and race, all swore by the *same* free-market theory down to the exact same assumptions. All shared disdain for identical institutions, especially the government. Instead of reading the economic classics to digest what Smith and Malthus actually said, they read their teachers' textbooks that interpreted what Smith and Malthus might have said.

III Understanding Idi Amin

The bogeyman of the Second American Empire was corruption, which by definition cast the state in the villain's role. This definition became an ideology with an axe to grind because corruption was defined with *only* the government in mind. Because the government was seen as being intrinsically corrupt, thinking of nothing other than "rent seeking," it was banished, while the private sector remained pure as fresh-fallen snow. This was a big mistake, because since the dawn of civilization, the public and private sectors have warranted equal monitoring. In Bombay in the *1870*s, "the textile industry seemed to exist for no other purpose than to support a gigantic system of swindling."[8] The private sector initiates bribery, creates scarcities to raise prices, cheats on taxes, misrepresents products, and doesn't pay wages.

Since governments in the Third World intervened everywhere, corruption was seen to exist everywhere. In fact, corruption *is* everywhere, whether governments intervene in markets or not. It can be found in the past and in the present. For example, "In an address to a Roman Emperor of about A.D. 390, Libanius describes how soldiers in rural billets are all 'on the take,' all selling 'protection' under their commanding officer against collectors of rents and taxes," which starved the cities of revenues for development.[9] Corruption can be found under capitalism and communism, in the North, the South, in every country, in every industry. Humans break laws—natural and unnatural—to satisfy their desires.

But some industries are very corrupt and some aren't, particularly the mid-tech industries that the developmental state promoted (steel, rubber tires, petrochemicals, machinery, and automobiles). Poorer countries have weaker institutions to deal with corruption than richer ones because legitimate roads to riches are few and far between, so corruption is greater in poorer countries. Sometimes corruption kills development and sometimes it coexists peacefully with it.

If corruption is not synonymous with the developmental state, then how can we put into perspective corruption's worst symbol, the murderous dictator Idi Amin?

A much-respected private detective on corruption, Transparency International, Inc., measures corruption according to the guesses, feelings, hunches, and assertions of more than 2,000 multinational firms that are interviewed. But relying on perceptions can be very misleading. An American might perceive bribing a public official in India as more corrupt than lobbying a legislator in Washington, but influence peddling in both cases may be the same. How about the opinions of the Third World's government officials, who deal on a daily basis with corrupt multinational firms? American multinationals are among the biggest lobbyists in the WTO. During trade negotiations in Doha in 2004, delegates from the South were disappointed that the United States "failed to address the issue of corrupt corporations, the vast funds they give to Congress and the White House to finance elections, and their ability to get laws written in their favor," all of which affect the WTO's decision-making process.[10] Business as usual in one setting may be corruption in another.

The major institutions that expose corruption all over the world are the press (private) and the courts (public). Both come out of "civil society" and have been an essential part of economic development. To shut down the developmental state is not only to lose momentum for development but also to lose the dynamism of these bodies as growth falters.

Poor countries that are rich in raw materials, such as Nigeria, are magnets for corruption. Every foreign company wants a license and every government official wants a bribe. But corruption in oil-producing countries that are OPEC members appears to have all but ceased. OPEC is professional, transparent, and good in accounting, and it makes public how much oil a country buys and sells. A comparable organization for Africa—say a group that could be called AMEC, African Metals Exporting Countries—would do wonders for revenues and foreign exchange. But the Second American Empire no more promoted the creation of such an organization than it supported OPEC.

Corruption is worst in the poorest countries without manufacturing experience, a robust press, or a judicial system. The corruption surrounding aid in these countries has all but killed the goose that lays the golden egg. Aid has to be tied to investment, and investment has to be made conditional on the productive use of aid. Otherwise, other Idi Amins will arise. Although Amin's brutal personality was noted when he first joined the British Colonial Army, the circumstances that enabled his regime put corruption into general perspective—where it comes from and how it survives. Amin was from a very poor country (Uganda), ruled when Africa was collapsing from debt, and operated in one of the South's most corrupt industries—the military.

IV The Most Variable Cost

Governments may be reluctant to restructure, like Japan in the 1990s after its financial bubble burst. The biggest fear is that restructuring will worsen unemployment—the other end of the spectrum from the "pink slip" model of firing workers. If employment has been maintained using protection, then the open market policy of the Second American Empire will reduce employment and affect a country's deepest social choices.

India and Egypt were wary of a ricochet effect if they restructured their huge textile industries because a change in one stage of production would trigger a change in other stages. If cheap synthetic yarn were imported, then the demand for raw cotton would fall, and so forth. Somewhere along the line of decision-making, the cost of greater efficiency was judged to be too high.

While still a fragile democracy in the 1960s, India openly and deliberately sacrificed economic efficiency for social harmony; as a result, millions of hand-loom weavers were saved: "In a labour abundant economy which already has a very high level of unemployment, any policy aimed at modernization requires careful consideration in view of its welfare implications."[11] In the 1960s the Indian government agreed to waive all restrictions on restructuring if modernized textile manufacturers agreed to a performance standard: export at least 50 percent of their output to relieve an acute shortage of foreign exchange, which could then create even more jobs. Few manufacturers took the bait because they didn't have the capital to restructure. On the other hand, restructuring in Korea and Taiwan, the big winners in textiles in the 1960s and 1970s, was financed by American aid. Neither country had to fire workers because all textile companies were new. In effect, India restructured along the lines of China: *restructuring was slow until alternative job opportunities expanded.*

Egypt's textile industry dates back to the nineteenth century and employs about one-fifth of Egypt's labor force in over 2,000 textile factories, many of which are state-owned lemons. Layoffs were inconceivable. The welfare tradition of the Egyptian government, as noted earlier, went back to the days of Nasser after his overthrow of King Farouk. Nasser and other young military officers desperately wanted to work with the private sector, and asked it for a list of demands. The officers' disappointment was bitter when they discovered that what Egyptian entrepreneurs wanted most were wage cuts and more freedom to fire. The public sector then ballooned.

Even in Latin America, where Washington found its keenest customers for liberalization, actual restructuring was rare at the industry level. The incentives were not there for entrepreneurialism. Mexico's banks, for example, were nationalized in the early 1980s at the taxpayers' expense to avert financial calamity. Then in the early 1990s they were reprivatized and sold by the government at favorable prices to national investors. Gradually, nationals resold them to foreign investors at higher prices. But ownership didn't seem to matter. Whether under state, national, or foreign ownership, banks were not restructured, and taxpayers suffered a staggering loss. In 2005, most banks still got at least 50 percent of their income from pushing paper—charging commissions for checks, for example—rather than from interest on loans for capital formation. In Argentina, the result of radical restructuring is "still not powerful enough to generate a new pattern of specialization for Argentine industry that could represent a sustainable long-term model of development."[12]

Wage cuts and layoffs became the rule. Out of a sample of 44 developing countries in the 1980s, real manufacturing wages rose in 10, stayed constant in 4, and *fell in 30*. A United Nations study in 2005 by the International Labor Organization reported that half the world's workers, 1.4 billion people—*the highest number ever recorded*—earned less than two dollars a day. In Argentina, wages in 1990 were one-third less than what they were in 1970. The percentage of households below the poverty line increased from 8 percent in 1980 to 27 percent in 1990, a year *before* Argentina's really serious financial crash. In Mexico, the index of real manufacturing wages fell from 127 in 1982 to 74 in 1999, the NAFTA decade. The "informal sector" everywhere swelled with the unemployed and, making matters worse, paid no taxes.

So, after all, most of the Third World's private sector did "restructure"—by *lowering real wages and employment.* But the money saved was paltry, what with an unlimited labor supply, no pensions, and puny health care. Although it is hazardous to guess, with some imagination, planning, and condition-free loans, most countries could conceivably have done a little better!

V Loosening Up

Whatever the century, imperialists have not spoken kindly about those whom they have imperialized (and vice versa). In the British Empire, "natives" were considered stupid and lazy, and racial epithets were common. In the First American Empire, they were nationalist, headstrong, and foolish. Under the Second American Empire, negative statements were no longer made, except perhaps for references to emerging markets rather than emerging economies. Instead, its accusations of stupidity and foolishness were reserved for the past. Asia included, developing countries were slandered for their *earlier* policies, notwithstanding the extraordinary growth rates they had achieved under them. As late as 1993, when the World Bank published its *East Asian Miracle* report, Asia was still being portrayed as cockeyed and ignorant of what might have happened *if* its markets had been freed to grow faster (or much slower!).

Counterfactual arguments are nothing more than guesses. It is impossible to predict what might have happened if something else had occurred. But pushing this line of reasoning as gospel allowed the Second American Empire to disparage past policies or reject them out of hand. The fact remains that under statist policies, on average, the Third World grew very fast, and under free-market policies, on average, it grew very slowly.

Without any opposition, theoretical or practical, the ideas of the Second American Empire became an upholstered ideology. The first place to look for the stagnation of the age is probably right here. Only when giants appeared on the earth and threatened the Second American Empire's life did ideology loosen a little.

10 The Devil Take the Hindmost

We are witnessing a global pattern of redistribution of power. The era of Eurocentric or western political domination in the history of mankind is coming to an end. In the years ahead, what we now call the developing countries will increase their share of the world's goods.... The people they represent will be increasingly literate, informed, and politically assertive.

Zbigniew Brzezinski, 1979, President Carter's National Security Adviser

I Two Blocs Are Better Than One

Edward Gibbon, in his classic study, attributes Rome's fall to "Immoderate Greatness," an idea with two crucial parts that, together, create a paradox. If an empire lacks "greatness," keeping its periphery poor and ignorant, why shouldn't it survive? There are no new competitors to challenge it. On the other hand, if an empire has greatness, from promoting economic development, then why won't new competitors awaken to challenge its rule?

Is global growth good or bad for an empire? Will China help or hurt the United States? Can we learn from history, even the seemingly remote history of the 1823 Monroe Doctrine? A lack of growth is always bad because political opposition arises. The opposition may lure the military into movements against it, and the opposition may win (as in Cuba and Vietnam). Or slow growth may raise risks for foreign investors (the Middle East's non-oil sectors), or reduce economic spillovers (did NAFTA help American workers?). Without some real economic benefits for the home team, the grandest empire can become effete. On the other hand, big growth and new competitors from the Third World may not necessarily hurt the First World. In fact, they may make it richer, even if it retires from the business of policing the world!

When Gibbon was writing in the eighteenth century about the fall of Rome, "decline" meant descending into barbarism, drinking blood like the Gauls, and destroying Roman civilization. But since at least the time of the Italian city-states, imperial decline has merely meant relinquishing *supreme* power. *Former empires remain rich.* Amsterdam, London, Paris, Tokyo, and even Rome, all former seats of empire, are all still prosperous and cosmopolitan. The penalty of decline at the hands of new competitors is the loss of absolute or supreme power, not the loss of power and wealth.

But history doesn't necessarily repeat itself. The Second American Empire has more soft and hard power than any empire in history. Maybe it will never decline. The world will simply grow older and more polarized. Or maybe the giants that have awakened since the First American Empire's rule will knock its wind out, but America will remain regal and rich. The big question is whether it is nimble enough to change.

If the past is any guide, what will matter for power and wealth are ideas and the institutions that nurture them, especially the institutions tied to income distribution and regional integration. China is tightly integrated economically with the rest of Asia, which makes it larger than life. It is also relatively egalitarian, although in the last few years of cowboy capitalism it has retreated from purist egalitarianism, where almost everyone's income was the same. Integration and equality have helped China build the nationally owned businesses that are necessary for intense global competition. The United States is rooted in Latin America, but the roots binding the hemisphere are weak and shallow. Latin America has become one of the slowest-growing regions in the world and one of the most unequal, dragging the United States under. There are few feisty Latin American multinationals to fight against China's new firms.

China and the United States will face each other as parts of regions, Asia and Latin America. Asia's ideas now emerge from an eclectic mixture of East, West, and a tiny bit of the former Soviet Union. Flexibility is prized. Confucianism means hard work, and the rest of its precepts have been banished to the family. In contrast, the ideas of the United States come out of the Enlightenment. In the counterculture, now slain, experimentation was prized. But in the culture that is now alive, the message is to stay the course: the American Empire will be sustained by free trade and free elections. Can this solution be peaceful for the world and positive for the United States?

II Income Equality

In the early stages of development, people fight over land and its associated industries—farming, fishing, ranching, and mining. Land distribution and its cousin, income distribution, tend to become highly unequal where population density is low and land is abundant, as in Latin America. In the eighteenth century, Argentina saw vast stretches of its pampas, or grazing land, being acquired by only a few families. In the United States, by contrast, the Homestead Act of 1862 gave 160 acres free to anyone who was willing to farm them for 5 years (40 acres plus a mule were supposed to be given to freed slaves, but this land reform was rescinded during Reconstruction). The land distribution index in 1960 was 0.86 in Argentina, 0.83 in Brazil, 0.35 in S. Korea, and 0.45 in Taiwan (the higher the number, the greater the inequality). By 1960, due to bankruptcies, mergers, and acquisitions, land distribution in the United States had also become unequal (0.71). In contrast, in postreform Japan, the measure of land distribution was only 0.41.

By the 1980s, income distribution in the South was being influenced by what happened in the urban sector, where industry tended to be located. But usually the influence of land on income distribution remained paramount. The ratio by which the income of the top fifth of the urban population exceeded that of the bottom fifth in 1986 to 1995 varied, but equality in Asia was greater than elsewhere and equality in Latin America was weak (again, a high number indicates inequality). The ratio was 28 in Brazil, 15 in Mexico, 10 in India, 8 in China, 5 in Korea, and 4 in Taiwan (data are from different sources and are not above suspicion). The income ratio was 11 in the United States and 4 in Japan.[1] Thus, the discrepancy in income distribution between Asia and Latin America—and their respective mentors, Japan and the United States—remains huge, although restructuring in the 1990s made income distribution more unequal even in Japan.

If land is unequally distributed, a few families get the best land in terms of arability, crop variety, irrigation, and access to markets. This gives them an above-average rate of profit. If land is divided into one huge ranch for a single family, instead of ten ranches for ten families, there is no market competition, and the profitability of the biggest ranch is also super-high. Large landholdings, and related agro-industries and banking, thus become a magnet for capital and for the educated sons and daughters of the elite, who work where returns are highest. There is no incentive for the rich to invest in the manufacturing industry because it is risky—experimentation is key to success—and it is hard work. Technological know-how spreads throughout the population at a snail's pace, and most jobs are unskilled and low paid, remaining in agriculture and mining. The demand for education is slowed by the absence of meritocracy. What matters is who owns what, not who does what.

The presence of rich natural resources may worsen the inequality in a country, but the effect of natural resources on equality depends on how they are distributed. Latin America's big landowners (latifundistas) don't even cultivate most of their land, for fear of driving up the demand for labor and the wages of their peasants. Compare the latifundistas with smaller owners of the same type of land in the United States, where agriculture follows modern management practices and scientific farming.

One of the highest costs of income inequality in developing countries is a stunted manufacturing sector. The big money goes to the haciendas, ranches, and mines, where monopoly power and profitability are high. Exceptions should be noted: Brazil, with one of the most unequal income distributions, had one of the largest manufacturing sectors, 26 percent of its GDP in 1990, compared with a manufacturing sector of 22 percent of GDP in Chile, 31 percent in South Korea, and 36 percent in Taiwan. Economists argue that it is immaterial to growth whether a country produces potato chips or computer chips, minerals or machine tools; profitability depends on market competition, not technology. But competition is likely to be less in computer chips because knowledge is a barrier to entry. Thus, profits will be higher, and wages are also likely to be much higher because skills are higher. For these reasons, the manufacturing sector is the heart of modern economic growth and social welfare. Out of it springs the middle class that tends to militate for political democracy.

Asia's income equality may be given partial credit for its outstanding entrepreneurship, education, emphasis on manufacturing, strong work ethic, productive agriculture, and toleration for fiscal discipline. The jury is out on its political stability. China and Myanmar are still undemocratic. But one form of political stability, crucial in early industrial transformation, has been far stronger in Asia than in Latin America: a professional bureaucracy to manage the process of economic change. Asia's bureaucracy continues to exist despite the Second American Empire's war against the state.

As Max Weber observed, a good bureaucracy is based on the principle of equality. Dating back to China's ancient dynasties, Asia has chosen its bureaucrats according to their performance on formal exams, not their political connections. The most brilliant and respected members of society become the highest civil servants. A decade ago, a brief survey of Korea's Ministry of Finance indicated that of the top ten bureaucrats (the minister and vice minister are political appointees), nine had graduated from Seoul National University (considered Korea's best academic institution) and one had graduated from Korea University (Korea's second-best academic institution). The U.S. Treasury, by contrast, is full of political appointees well down the hierarchical ladder. In China and its neighbors, political appointees stop with the minister and vice minister. Everyone else is a professional.

The "iron cage" of bureaucracy may stultify originality, but it is fair and egalitarian, whether in China, India, Korea, Taiwan, or Thailand, and lends a professionalism to policy making that is weaker in Africa, the Middle East, Latin America, and the United States.

With its top-notch civil servants and penchant for manufacturing, in the absence of any other domestic investment opportunities, Asia surged ahead of Latin America in the 1980s. A comparison of Chile and Taiwan again illustrates the point. Both countries are about the same size in terms of population and geographical area, and both have especially prosperous agricultures. But Chile has a big state-owned copper-mining industry (Chile mined silver under the Spaniards) and a highly unequal income distribution, not to mention a bloody 1973 coup d'etat and a record of "missing persons" on its hands. Taiwan's income distribution, by contrast, is highly equal, and its manufacturing sector excels by world standards, although Taiwan's history also includes four decades of martial law, and sometimes violent tensions between the old Nationalist government and native Taiwanese. The share of manufactures in total exports in 1995 was 93 percent in Taiwan and only 14 percent in Chile. Taiwan's population growth was fast, but manufacturing investments absorbed it. Although Chile was Latin America's economic star, Taiwan still outshone it. In 1973 Taiwan's per capita income was only a fraction of Chile's (73 percent), whereas by 1995 Chile's per capita income was only a fraction of Taiwan's (68 percent as much).

The slow, seesaw growth of the Latin American region is becoming a major liability to the United States in its confrontation with Asia, not least of all because of U.S. trade policies. The slower Latin America's growth, which now depends on China's demand for raw materials, the slower the growth in demand for U.S. products and in the supply of profitable investment opportunities for American firms. Migration from Latin America to the United States increases, which puts a drag on American wages. The poor in Latin America are forced to migrate—14.1 percent of the U.S. population is now Latino.

Equality is a big asset for a developing country. Its returns range from a more cohesive population to more powerful manufacturing firms.

III Roko D. Rockefeller

The ownership of a firm doesn't matter at the bottom of the technological ladder—the more foreign and local investment the better. But once an economy reaches toward mid-technology industries, national ownership becomes a big plus.

Table 10.1
The R&D Rat Race

Country	Expenditure for R&D as Percent of GDP, 1996–2002
Developing Countries	
Korea	2.53
Singapore	2.15
China	1.23
Brazil	1.04
India	.85
South Africa	.67
Turkey	.66
Developed Countries	
Israel	5.08
Sweden	4.27
Finland	3.46
Japan	3.12
USA	2.66
Switzerland	2.57
Germany	2.53

Source: *World Development Report* Development Indicators (World Bank, 2005).

When a landmark American firm is being taken over by a foreign firm in an election year, the floor shakes in the Committee on Foreign Investments: Dubai's takeover of terminal operations at six American ports was prevented by Congress (although China operates most U.S. ports on the West Coast); Rockefeller Center's takeover by Japan was lamented, but Dubai's takeover of the Essex House was ignored; Chrysler's takeover by Daimler-Benz from Germany was deplored; and the acquisition of a U.S. energy company, Unocal, by China's state-owned CNOOC was stopped despite China's earlier assumption of control of IBM's personal computer business. Europe behaves the same way as the United States, raising hell when an unwanted foreign suitor appears: Mittal Steel, a Dutch company owned by Indians, was thwarted by France from buying the French steel giant Arcelor; Suez and Gaz de France merged to thwart a takeover by the Italian Enei. Russia's Gazprom was barred from buying the British natural gas company Centrica. Most of this happened around 2005, when cheers for globalization were being heard around the world.

If the European Union and United States sing the praises of foreign investment to developing countries, why do they do an about-face to protect certain of their own assets, even if they ignore the thousands of ordinary takeovers by foreign firms that never get reported?

One reason is nationalism. Another reason is the popular sense that a country gets more from a first-rate firm when its ownership is national than when its ownership is foreign. *Nothing could be truer than this popular feeling when it comes to national ownership in developing countries, depending on the industry.* In low-tech, labor-intensive industries, where each firm allegedly faces an infinite demand for its product, nationalism is unnecessary. Developing countries should warmly welcome foreign firms in these industries, following the example in the 1960s of Korea and Taiwan. There is plenty of room for foreign *and* domestic firms in low-skilled industries because world demand and the domestic labor supply are almost unlimited—garments, candles, and cooking ware are examples. These industries create employment and diffuse management know-how that can be used in other industries. They take the sting off unemployment and social unrest.

But in mid-tech and high-tech industries, foreign firms crowd out nationally owned firms. Because there is a scarcity of know-how and demand, entry is limited. Foreign firms have more experience, brand-name recognition, and technological finesse. Yet there are good reasons to keep foreign firms out of mid-tech sectors until domestic firms catch up.

There are four advantages to national ownership in developing countries. First, multinational firms that operate in developing countries are all identical; the best and the brightest personnel are kept at corporate headquarters. Subsidiaries tend to operate bureaucratically and are slow to market. In contrast, nationally owned firms tend to be more entrepreneurial and fast on their feet. By the early 1980s, Hyundai Motors was certainly outperforming Daewoo Motors, a joint venture between a Korean company and General Motors. Hyundai, member of a big Korean conglomerate, excelled in growth rate, productivity, exports, and nurturing local parts and components suppliers.[2]

Second, under national ownership, any entrepreneurial rents or technological profits stay in the developing country rather than being repatriated overseas. The skills that generate such profits are also present; they can be used locally again and again; CEOs (chief executive officers); COOs (chief operating officers); CFOs (chief financial officers), and so on. If ownership is foreign, these highest skills and fattest profits are never kept at home. By comparison, big nationally owned firms, most of them business groups, are a laboratory for creating managers. The Samsung group in Korea hired its managers centrally, at corporate headquarters. After managers of the same training class got to know each other, they were dispersed to subsidiaries in different industries. Every manager then had personal contacts in every other affiliate, creating good communication. The idea that premier local managers were in scarce supply was soon outdated; they were trained, used, and reused in different industries, unlike the multinationals, which are specialized and never transfer managers to different industries.

Third, because the best and the brightest in a multinational remain at home, especially in corporate research labs, R&D investments in developing countries are more glitter than gold. The best projects are kept under the eye of top management and guarded by the technical elite in headquarters. For example, although General Electric talked up its lab in Bangalore, with 600 workers, that lab could never replicate the work that GE was doing in its corporate lab in Schenectady, New York, with 2,000 to 3,000 workers. The corporate lab was doing advanced research, using advanced math, while the Bangalore lab was doing applied research using algorithmic math.

Fourth, globalization in the form of *outward* investment helps a company see the road map of its industry and what competitors in other countries are doing. But a country can't globalize by investing overseas if it doesn't have its own companies. It is silly to speak of a foreign company globalizing from a foreign country. If GE opens a factory in Pakistan, it is globalizing from the United States, not from India, because GE is an American company. The difference in outward investment between Asia and Latin America has a long history. From 1986 to 1991, according to the UN's foreign investment report, outward foreign investment (in $U.S. million) was only $634 for Latin America (Argentina, Brazil, Chile, and Mexico), mostly to other Latin American countries, and $4,432 for Asia (Korea, Taiwan, Malaysia, and Indonesia). It was $745 for China. In 1997, before the dot-com U.S. boom and bust, outward foreign investment was $4,583 for the same four Latin American countries, $16,896 for the same four Asian countries, and $2,500 for China. Globalization of investment was thus almost four times as great in Asia as in Latin America.

IV Decolonization's Heavy Inheritance

National ownership was the offspring of decolonization, one of the great historical movements after World War II. Decolonization followed the rise of national independence struggles (the bloodiest were in Algeria, China, Indonesia, Kenya, and Vietnam). Independence was promoted by the First American Empire, which was being urged by domestic protest movements to end colonialism and pressured by the State Department and Treasury to free the colonial markets controlled by France and the United Kingdom. But not every developing country gained independence after World War II. Most of Latin America had won its political freedom from Spain and Portugal much earlier, in the 1820s. Latin American countries, therefore, missed the upheavals, cleansing, and redistributive effects of postwar decolonization.

When a colony is freed, it kicks out the old guard, often including *foreign-owned firms*. If foreign governments go, foreign firms typically flee. After the Communist Revolution, China expropriated Japan's heavy manufacturing in Manchuria, which is the basis today of China's national automobile and coal-mining industries. Even Japan's trolley cars are still running on northern China's city streets. When the Raj exited India, many British firms took flight, or couldn't compete against Indian firms and went bankrupt. When the Indonesians finally expelled the Dutch in 1953, they inherited over 400 mixed enterprises, ranging from banks to factories to mines. When Japan was driven from Korea by the Allied forces in the Pacific, it left behind manufacturing plants in varying degrees of disarray, including a major shipyard and a modern cement mill. It also left a functioning banking system with a "five main bank" structure employing well-trained Korean bureaucrats.

If locals had the expertise to operate abandoned properties, newly independent countries got a head start. More important, decolonization gave them a breathing space. Foreign firms, with their experience, political connections, and global presence, were no longer around to dominate the market and suffocate national start-ups. Laws were passed that prevented the return of foreign big business, like IBM in India and Japanese textile firms in Korea. *The absence of "crowding out" enabled nationally owned firms to enter and ultimately to control mid-tech sectors*. Examples are pulp and paper, automobiles, steel, petrochemicals, shipbuilding, and services such as banking, insurance, and telecommunications.

Without decolonization to free Latin America of foreign ownership, its nationally owned firms faced far more competition than Asian firms faced. The first multinational, Pirelli, invested in Argentina in 1917, and foreign firms just kept coming. They already monopolized many of the mid-tech industries that nationals could conceivably have entered after the war. In the 1950s, the First American Empire encouraged the Frondizi government in Argentina to actively recruit foreign firms. As early as 1977, the share of American investors in total Latin American industry was 23 percent in nonelectrical machinery, 31 percent in electrical machinery, and as much as 65 percent in transport equipment (cars, trucks, buses). The average foreign share in manufacturing was 20 percent. At the time, Asia had almost no foreign investors to speak of, either American or Japanese. The decks were cleared for Asians to build their own big businesses, with the Japanese *zaibatsu* as their model.

Latin America has plenty of first-rate nationally owned firms, from Brazil's formerly state-owned Embraer (aerospace) to Mexico's Cemex (cement). But Latin America has few global enterprises that can support America in taking on most of the new competitors in Asia. The United States now has a huge trade deficit with Asia. Ideally, it should have a huge trade surplus with Latin America, which, in turn, should have a huge trade surplus with Asia, through the sale of raw materials. But this triangular trade doesn't exist because Latin America's import capacity is feeble. In 2005, the U.S. trade balance with Latin America was negative, almost $100 billion, with Mexico accounting for about half the deficit. Because Latin America's absorptive capacity was small and it couldn't buy many U.S. goods, there was little relief for the $805.2 billion U.S. trade deficit.

V From Riches to Rags

When Latin America emerged from World War II, it was the richest region in the developing world. By the 1980s, Asia had overtaken it in per capita income, exports, and even poverty alleviation. Over the course of the 1990s, according to the UN *Human Development Report* (2002), the share of the population earning less than $1.00 a day barely changed in Latin America, while in East Asia it fell by half. What happened?

Part of the blame lies in Latin America's land distribution dating to the Portuguese and Spanish conquest: historically, Latin America's distribution of land, income, and wealth has been one of the most unequal in the world, inhibiting knowledge-based investments by the super-rich. Another part of the blame comes from missing the cleansing effects of decolonization: without land reform, without the flight of foreign firms, and without the creation of a critical, minimum number of professionally managed national companies, Latin America was unable to exercise its skills to survive in a high-tech world. Growth has taken the form of spurts and slumps, but on average, as Latin America has followed its northern leader down the path of liberalization, its growth in income, employment, regional trade, and technology has stagnated.

The Second American Empire's agenda—privatization, deregulation, and liberalization— hit Latin America especially hard, given the tight knot between the United States and Latin America since the Monroe Doctrine. Privatization in Latin America created more foreign takeovers in industry and finance, often fanning the flames of inflation. Deregulation allowed the completely free movement of "hot" money and cold-hearted loan pushers, which enabled contagious region-wide debt crises, beginning with Mexico in 1982. Later, East Asia fell into a debt trap as well. But East Asia's stumble was due to overproduction, while Latin America's was due to irresponsible regulatory policies. The "free" trade agreements that the United States signed with Mexico (1991) and Central America (2006) outlawed state-led restructuring as the price of accessing a tariff-free U.S. market. The factories that Latin America had built under the First American Empire needed sprucing up, but antistatism squelched the rebuilding of companies with state money and coordination.

The developmental state that flourished during the First American Empire was killed, with nothing workable to replace it. Although the theory of open markets is unquestionably logical, it meant little because its assumptions were invalid in the South, and its implementation by the Second American Empire was rigid, opportunistic, and devoid of creative ideas and practical policies. Latin America's economy began playing second string in the developing world, weakening the whole Western Hemisphere. Asia, with its giant share of the world's population, began taking a giant share of world markets as well, a convergence of population and power that Arnold J. Toynbee foresaw. After the Second American Empire took its share, the Latin American people had to fend for themselves. "The devil take the hindmost."

11 Great Balls of Fire

Revenge is a dish best served cold.

Italian proverb

I Power

Nearly overnight, yet almost imperceptibly, American's deeds in the developing world became subject to a veto by "giants." Some giants have a mixture of low wages, huge populations, high skills, heavy investments in technical education and R&D, and activist states that keep markets flying. For example, China and India combine low wages with large numbers of world-class managers and engineers. These super-giants have big domestic markets along with large armies. Any infringement on their strategic interests—including oil—may now be met with a credible deterrent. Giants are the "Great Balls of Fire" that are setting the world ablaze. *This is the immediate meaning behind America's loss of absolute power.*

For the second time in modern history (the first time was in Vietnam), the threat to absolutism comes from below, from among less developed countries trying to catch up, not from above, from other imperialists. Thus, the world has truly changed, probably for the best. There can be no imperial greatness without economic development, and if greatness slides into immoderation, the empire will perish in the turbulent waters, dry deserts, and unsanitary slums of the developing world.

To its credit, the Second American Empire has approached China peacefully. Beijing and Washington have engaged in ultrasecret "strategic" talks to smooth out their differences over who gets what. Given peace, what will matter is mastery in the marketplace.

Compared to China, the United States starts from way ahead in economic power, in terms of the size of its economy (measured in GNP), its large international class of techno-financial whiz kids, its national innovation system, its multinational firms, its unrivaled higher education, and its Wall Street bankers, hedge fund managers, and venture capitalists. China's advantages are a raging growth rate and a population that is raring to go. China can brag about rising employment and plummeting poverty. It has an ultrahigh savings rate (35 to 40 percent), a bureaucracy chosen by a meritocratic exam system, and entrepreneurial big-business groups. China is now a growth model admired by would-be giants for its flexibility. Neither India nor China (nor Taiwan) deregulated their financial markets to inflows and outflows of capital, and neither ever succumbed to a debt crisis: it was too risky to experiment with a billion people.

Politically, a giant and an empire are strangers, at opposite ends of the power grid. China is dictatorial at home but relatively peaceful overseas. It conquered Tibet; it helped Vietnam on the battlefield and later invaded it; and it insists on governing Hong Kong and Taiwan. But Chinese aggrandizement has not crept much beyond Asia. China's military power is still parochial, as is India's, while an imperial power like the United States has the world as its oyster: its conquests may occur on the other side of the earth, or on the moon. For most of the postwar years, the United States was all-powerful because it had advanced technology *and* a big immigrant population. It also had "soft power"—English became the universal language; everybody wore American fashions; everybody ate American fast foods; and everybody watched American movies, listened to American music, and copied the American suburbs. Unlike the empire of Alexander the Great, which conquered only *part* of the developing world, the United States has indirectly ruled nearly *all* of it! According to the U.S. Defense Department's *Base Structure Report*, in around 2005 the Pentagon had over 700 bases in roughly 130 countries. In addition, it is building 14 "enduring bases" for long-term encampment in Iraq, and provided military education and training to 113 countries. The magnitude of these numbers is apparent by comparing them with UN membership—191 countries, many of them tiny.

But powers in the past have been undone by their own devices, and military bases have vanished like castles in the sand.

China has a golden egg that the United States doesn't come close to having. It is part of a fast-growing region whose growing cohesiveness elicits a cool response on the part of the United States: "While an important element in Europe's integration was strong American support, it is unlikely that the United States will support East Asian regionalism."[1] When Malaysian Prime Minister Mahathir Muhamad proposed a regional currency arrangement, the U.S. opposed it because it would lead to an Asia-only grouping. When Japan proposed an Asian IMF, Washington nixed it because it was excluded. Nevertheless, this lack of American encouragement didn't hurt Asian cooperation. Even ignoring the benefits of trade and investment, regionalism provides Asian countries with invaluable information about each other, from the width of the aisles in Hyundai's car plants (of interest to China's nascent automobile industry) to the way Japan pumps out exports, the 24-karat gold of the whole region.

Asian countries have had crisscross trade ties with each other since at least the nineteenth century. In contrast, Latin American countries hardly trade with each other except in a colonial pattern, North and South. Imports and exports, air flights, and finance flow through Miami. The United States should *strengthen Latin America so it can lock horns with Asia*; otherwise, China won't face enough real competition, and Latin America will continue to fall. Latin America's exports of raw material to China help, trade between Argentina and Brazil is growing, and the awakening of a Brazilian giant would make matters easier. But to beef up Latin America requires establishing an unorthodox Marshall Plan, at a time when few agencies in Washington convey a sense of openness to any unorthodoxy. This is the most serious problem of current American foreign economic policy compared with that of the past.

The final question then becomes: *What has made the Second American Empire so rigid by previous imperial standards*? Or, why does Washington cram the same rules, laws, and institutions down the throats of all developing countries that can't—or choose not to—escape? This question is especially puzzling since long ago, under GATT, the whole world drifted toward free trade, and tariffs fell sharply. It is not as though Third World tariffs didn't decline at all, or shift from old to new industries. Arguably, the North, not the South, is the spoiler. By the 1990s, most African countries supported free trade in order to export their cotton, corn, sugar, and rice to Japan, the United States, and Europe, but trade barriers stopped them and snipped their life support. What the Third World opposes is not open markets in goods—the conventional meaning—but the invasion of open markets into their corporate boards, banks, foreign-investment rules, convenience stores, state-owned enterprises, water systems, telecommunication services, factories, and living rooms.

Anti-imperialist passions aren't worn by giants on their sleeve and many American- and British-trained local professionals are ultra-free traders. But disappointment is engraved in their minds. Revenge, as the proverb goes, is a dish best served cold.

II Heaven Learns about Laissez-Faire

The First American Empire's interpretation of laissez-faire as "do it *your* way" was exceptional for its freeness. It came close to the conventional meaning of the Enlightenment economists—"let them do"—but this nineteenth-century version had markets in mind: let markets do their thing without government meddling. Instead, the First American Empire had institutions in mind: institutions may have to deviate from a dogmatic ideal to create a growth engine with more horsepower than the market. The British Empire had effectively defined laissez-faire as "do as little as decency allows," as in India, and eventually crumbled. With the rise of the Second American Empire, laissez-faire's definition became harsher than ever: "do it *our* way." Growth rates sputtered, and U.S. power began to wane.

The low-key definition of the First American Empire was understandable, given the bewildering array of new countries it faced after decolonization. Instead of imposing one policy on all, Washington awarded the Marshall Plan to Europe, and gave Third World countries the leeway to design and execute their own development plans, their own mix of public and private, and their own regulation of industry—as long as they steered clear of communism. This wasn't the first time the United States had turned its back to good effect. After Admiral Perry's opening of Japan in 1868, the United States let Tokyo ponder its own rite of passage.

Countries embarking on their own development a century later also "did it their own way," as Japan had. Those with enough prewar manufacturing experience began to industrialize at breakneck speed (Brazil, Chile, Mexico, Turkey, India, China, Indonesia, Korea, Malaysia, Taiwan, and Thailand), using "unpackaged" technology. Such technology wasn't the property of a multinational firm competing against them in their own industry. Instead, know-how came from outside their industry—from their consultants, retirees, and suppliers of parts and machinery, who were uninhibited in providing them with a road map of where their technology was likely to go. This "unpackaging" in industries such as steel, pulp and paper, textiles, and automobiles helped the Third World establish its own national enterprises. Especially lucky in this regard were countries that had gone through postwar decolonization. The process of decolonization usually meant the flight of foreign governments *and foreign firms*, making room for domestic firms to grow in industries with large economies of scale. China expropriated foreign firms, India frightened them away, and Korea and Taiwan gathered what Japan had quickly left behind, such as a well-greased banking system. The least lucky was Latin America, where decolonization had occurred a century earlier, and sleepy multinational subsidiaries from Europe and the United States hung on after World War II. National firms in Asia grew brick by brick, machinery supplier by machinery supplier, subsidy by subsidy, entrepreneurial decision by entrepreneurial decision. The creation of professionally managed, family-owned firms, with an entrepreneurial dynamo on top, was probably the hardest step to make in modern economic development, and became a joint effort between business and government. Only with nationally owned firms was globalization possible in the form of outward foreign investment. Thus were born fresh competitors for the multinational Cadillacs of this world.

The First American Empire presided over a Golden Age, with a hot sun baking on all regions. Some regions, without a protective cover, got a raw sunburn. Others, with experience in sunbathing, got a beautiful tan.

Generally, the more freedom it has to determine its own policies, the faster a developing country will grow. The more manufacturing experience a developing country has accumulated, including higher education, and the more performance standards it attaches to state subsidies, the stronger it will develop economically without experiencing corruption. The accumulation of manufacturing experience before World War II was a twist of fate: when confronted with the prospect of Japanese invasion, the European empires began to mobilize their colonies for war, including war-related industries. Business people in Korea, Japan's colony, cheered when Japan invaded Manchuria, in anticipation of wartime profits. China and India had large industries begun in the nineteenth century, ranging from textiles to steel, that were started by local entrepreneurs with foreign technical assistance. Argentina, Brazil, Chile, and Mexico also got their manufacturing experience from foreign immigrants. There is no evidence of a poor country either leapfrogging to riches with a rush toward free markets or becoming democratic overnight. *As economic development produces a larger and larger middle class, from petty merchants to professional managers, democracy has a better chance of taking root.* Thus, laissez-faire works best when it means "do your own thing."

III China Is Big, Asia Is Bigger

Affiliation to a dynamic regional bloc can make an empire or giant larger than life because growth tends to spread within one region before it spreads to other regions, as was first observed in Europe. European development was like a dot of ink spreading on a blotter, with the development of one country scaring other countries into modernizing.[2] As early as 1830, 68 percent of Europe's trade was estimated to have been internal, rising to 80 percent by 1990.

China is vast, but as an integral part of rapidly growing Asia, it is even vaster. *By 2005, over 50 percent of China's imports came from Asia; only 10 percent came from the United States.* China imported more from Asia than it exported to it, thus running a trade deficit. However, China's inward foreign investment is not the big American feast it's made out to be, given that "overseas Chinese," mostly from Hong Kong and Taiwan, account for more than half of long-term capital flowing into China.

In a slow-growing region such as Africa, ambitious countries like South Africa and southern Nigeria may face a harder time industrializing than if they were located in a fast-growing region. Neighboring countries learn from each other, fearful that they might otherwise fall behind. Regionalism shields countries from global instability and gives companies a boost overseas, as everyone gets to know the name and quality of a region's products. For example, Korea could sell its cars in Eastern Europe after the collapse of communism because buyers initially thought they were made in Japan. Regional integration also encourages specialization and the division of labor, as extolled by Adam Smith. Thus, we're seen Asia become a hub of the electronics industry. Regional proximity saves time and transportation costs, although these costs have fallen dramatically over time. When a technical problem is next door, "after-sales service" is quicker and more efficient. Familiarity also makes finance smoother to arrange, since common legal and accounting systems reduce misunderstandings. And, if costs are competitive with those of the rest of the world, there is no danger of overpricing.

Asia's integration became tighter after the death of Mao in 1976 and the rise of Deng Xiaoping. China realized that it had fallen behind other Asian countries economically. The story is that Deng was on a train to Beijing and saw a Chinese-American teenager walking down the aisle wearing a digital watch around her neck. Deng and his associates examined it and realized that China was behind technologically. Learning was made easier by the fact that Chinese people had long migrated to other parts of Asia and had formed a network with whom China could communicate. As a result, a reporter wrote in 2006, "China is driving intra-Asian economic integration through the Association of Southeast Asian Nations, *which excludes the United States and Japan*. By 2010 the region's trade with China is likely to outstrip its trade with the United States."[3]

The United States promoted East Asian development unintentionally. In order to become less dependent on the American market, and not be besieged by demands from Washington to "Buy American" and help decrease the U.S. trade deficit, Korea began to "Sell Asian." As a total of Korea's exports, those to Asia (excluding Japan) went from 7 percent in 1970 to around 35 percent in 2000.[4] So great was the desire of the Korean government to escape U.S. leverage that it offered subsidies to Korean companies that diversified the direction of their exports away from the United States. An elder Japanese statesman, Kiyoshi Kojima, stated that the United States had overstepped the bounds in pushing Asia for fast trade liberalization that only benefited American business. Most Asian countries "insisted that regional integration focus primarily on the promotion of economic development, and that trade liberalization should be promoted gradually."[5]

The Second American Empire wanted individual Asian countries to sign a free trade agreement with the United States. There were almost no free trade agreements in Asia at the beginning of the 1990s. Then, ASEAN, or the Association of South-East Asian Nations—Indonesia, Malaysia, Philippines, Singapore, Thailand (joined 1967), Brunei (1984), Vietnam (1995), Myanmar, Laos (1997), and Cambodia (1999)—which excludes the United States, began to sign agreements individually and collectively with Washington, with an eye on competing against the European Union and NAFTA. In March 2006, the Indian prime minister, Manmohan Singh, remarked in a speech to the Asia Society in Mumbai:

Table 11.1
Direction of Chinese Exports

Destination	Percentage of Total
Manufactured Exports (1995)	
United States	1%
Japan	2.5%
East Asian bloc (rest)	44.2%
Manufactured Exports (2000)	
United States	15.9%
Japan	15.8%
East Asian bloc (rest)	24.9%
Chemical Exports (1995)	
United States	9.8%
Japan	15%
East Asian bloc (rest)	27%
Chemical Exports (2000)	
United States	14.4%
Japan	14.1%
East Asian bloc (rest)	21%

Source: UN Comtrade database, http://libraries.mit.edu/guides/subjects/data/access/subject/trade/index.html.

> The process of engagement in the Asian region has truly taken off. I am confident it will be self-sustaining.... We are linking India into a web of partnerships with the countries of the region through free trade and economic cooperation agreements. We have concluded Free Trade Agreements with SAARC [South Asian Association for Regional Cooperation], Singapore, Thailand and ASEAN. We are working on similar arrangements with Japan, China and Korea. This web of engagements may herald an eventual free trade area in Asia covering all major Asian economies and possibly extending to Australia and New Zealand. This Pan Asian FTA could be the future of Asia.[6]

As India strengthened its "Look East" policy, the East was strengthened.

The rise of an Asian trade bloc between 1970 and 2000 is suggested in table 11.2. The share of regional exports for Taiwan doubled, from 20 percent to in 1970 to almost 40 percent in 2000, and it rose by about 50 percent in Malaysia and Indonesia. In 2004, Indonesian exports to China increased over the previous year by 232 percent. The share of exports to Asia circa 2000 was over 35 percent for Indonesia and Thailand, and 44 percent for Malaysia. Of India's total exports, Asia took 10 percent in 1970, 21

Table 11.2
Direction of Trade

From	Exports To		
Argentina	USA	Europe	Local
1970	10.3	55.5	21.1
1980	10.5	31.9	24.5
1995	10.8	22.5	47.2
2000	18.1	19.8	39.1
Brazil	USA	Europe	Local
1970	26.2	43.5	11.7
1980	18.6	32.2	18.1
1995	11.8	27.9	23.3
2000	23.4	24.4	23.3
Chile	USA	Europe	Local
1970	14.4	30.9	11.5
1980	11.5	41.7	24.7
1995	13.2	27.0	10.9
2000	18.1	24.3	21.7
Mexico	USA	Europe	Local
1970	71.2	11.1	10.5
1980	66.0	16.2	6.9
1995	86.2	5.0	6.1
2000	86.7	4.2	3.8
India	E. Europe	Europe	Local
1970	20.4	20.1	10.0
1980	20.3	25.3	10.7
1995	0.5	21.1	20.9
2000	2.6	23.0	31.8
China	Japan	USA	Local
1970	–	–	–
1985	22.3	8.6	36.5
1995	19.1	16.6	37.3
2000	16.7	20.9	31.1
Indonesia	Japan	USA	Local
1970	33.3	14.1	21.4
1980	41.3	11.8	16.7
1995	27.1	14.7	33.5
2000	23.2	14.3	38.1

Table 11.2
(continued)

From	Exports To		
Korea	Japan	USA	Local
1970	27.7	41.4	7.0
1980	17.3	28.4	14.7
1995	13.7	21.5	34.3
2000	11.9	23.4	35.1
Malaysia	Japan	USA	Local
1970	18.3	20.9	33.1
1980	22.8	18.0	33.3
1995	12.7	14.2	44.4
2000	13.0	21.4	44.1
Taiwan	Japan	USA	Local
1970	15.1	46.4	20.3
1980	11.0	36.6	17.7
1995	11.8	25.0	40.7
2000	11.2	23.5	38.7
Thailand	Japan	USA	Local
1970	26.3	13.6	30.7
1980	15.3	13.2	26.9
1995	16.8	19.0	35.5
2000	14.7	17.2	35.8

Local is defined for each country as follows (according to UNCTAD classifications): Other developing America: for Argentina, Brazil, Chile, Mexico. Other East Asia (including Hong Kong): for China, Indonesia, Korea, Malaysia, Taiwan, and Thailand. Other West Asia and East Asia: for India.

Source: United Nations Conference on Trade and Development; Amsden (2001).

percent in 1995, and just over 30 percent in 2000. In Latin America, by contrast, only Argentina had a high percentage of its (stagnating) exports going to other Latin American countries (47 percent in 1995). For Brazil, Chile, and Mexico, the figures in 1995 were 23 percent, 11 percent, and 6 percent, respectively.

China made new friends, however bitter the past. According to Singapore's *Straits Times*, China has turned on the charm in Indonesia, transforming a relationship that was once fraught with suspicion into a blossoming economic partnership. China's state energy companies have bought into Indonesian oil and natural gas fields in Java and Papua and are expected to bid on tenders for new power plants.[7] The ancient aversions that Asian countries had toward each other may now be less prevalent than the idea of an Asian bloc.

IV Heaven Hates Headstrongness

When the United States was isolationist before World War II, it took no responsibility for the Third World. But when it assumed power after World War II, responsibility for the Third World fell into its lap, and it was presented with a choice. On the one hand, the United States could control the Third World politically while doing next to nothing for it economically, as the French and British empires had more or less done. The cost of this decision was spending big money on maintaining law and order. Colonial history shows the desperation of this approach, which now seems to be getting more dire, with prisons for drunks being replaced by prisons for armed guerrillas. Alternatively, the United States could take responsibility for Third World economic development, as both the First and Second American Empires tried to do. One cost of being hands-on was coping with the Idi Amins of poor and institutionally impoverished countries, where corruption was extreme, sometimes rising, sometimes falling. But complexity, not simplicity, has characterized the relationship between corruption and growth. Corruption in many Third World countries was extreme under the First American Empire, as in Korea and Taiwan, where growth became electric, as well as under the Second American Empire, when growth in Africa and the Middle East burned out. Corruption is a way of life around the world, whether under communism and capitalism, and whether it's called looting or lobbying, but its destructiveness depends on the institutions that are built to contain it. Corruption may be compatible with growth or incompatible, but it is generally least destructive, as under the First American Empire, when successful development policies put it under lock and key.

Americans are responsible for Third World development because ultimately the quality of their own lives depend on it. Empires typically tyrannize the world around them while submitting sheepishly to powerful interest groups at home, because the only rationale for an empire's existence is the preservation of its own base. In the United States, business was Washington's liveliest lobby and biggest beneficiary. It was nothing out of the usual for a U.S. trade representative—under President Clinton—to become a power broker in Washington for Morgan Stanley, a Wall Street icon. Business in the United States had become "big" as early as the 1880s, before government became "big" in the 1930s—government expanded, measured by the size of the executive building, to fight the Great Depression and mobilize for war. Because business came first, it dug in its heels. Only when business was blamed for the stock market crash of 1929 did its reputation falter.

Not long after the Depression, business was again opening Washington's pockets. The United States laid on foreign aid to win the Cold War, but tied 80 percent of it to purchases from American firms. Aid was generous to countries threatened by communism, such as South Korea and Taiwan, but mainly for defense. Latin America was denied any aid whatsoever, and had to get its capital from multinational investments. Around the world, whatever old the United States gave was tied to the interests of its industries. Although the United States gave poor countries food aid, this aid helped big American farmers to off-load their surpluses. The United States championed decolonization, but this enabled American business to operate in the former monopolies of Britain and France. The United States offered Europe the Marshall Plan, but first hoped that Europe's colonies would pay for reconstruction! The United States talked democracy, but in 1954 overthrew a democratic Guatemalan president to help the United Fruit Company. And, although the United States allowed developing countries to slap tariffs on their industries, this policy helped American multinationals investing in those industries.

All the same, despite bowing to business, the First American Empire could still allow the developing world to "do it their way" because the power of American business was *relatively* weak. As mentioned earlier, Roosevelt called business and its cronies the "Royalists," and fought with them over government's economic role. The New Deal and World War II dramatized the importance of planning, and legalized trade unions. When Eisenhower left office in 1960, he (or a speech writer) expressed anxiety about the military-industrial complex. A healthy distance between business and government continued apace because investments by American multinationals in overseas manufacturing were still small. The closing bell only sounded when a famous French journalist, Jean-Jacques Servan-Schreiber, complained in 1967 of the domination of French industry by American multinationals (in his *Le défi américain*).

As memories of the 1930s faded, American business became empowered as never before. Wall Street went global big-time during the 1970s oil boom, asking Washington to end country-specific financial regulations that restricted its lending. The multinationals had arrived in Third World industries in the late 1960s. When U.S. assemblers of automobiles or electronics wanted to cut costs, they asked Washington to help open markets in the country in which they were locating in order to import their parts and components from other overseas subsidiaries. The information revolution deified the young, entrepreneurial innovator, who wanted Washington to enforce strict intellectual property rights. Forget about tariff protection for learning.

American foreign economic policy became increasingly one-sided as business and government shared an unshakable faith in free markets. What's good enough for American business became good enough for the Third World, even if leading Third World businesses became American-owned as a consequence.

V The Grand Finale: The Sleuth Reenters Earth

The sleuth of this book, first skulking around the Introduction, has now returned from Heaven and Hell for the grand finale. She is peering into two large crystal balls, one a magic ball belonging to the empire, and the other a great ball of fire belonging to the giants. Shadows from the balls overlap, casting a glow reserved for the First American Empire. This empire has a Golden Age of economic development under its belt due to its agility in navigating between state intervention and market forces, from the crudest intrusiveness in Third World politics to the freest meaning of laissez-faire, "do it *your* way." The First American Empire died in Vietnam from immoderation, which also brought down Rome, but it had lifted all boats in stormy seas, earning it the approbation of "greatness."

Now we see in the magic ball the Second American Empire. It is standing still. It stays inert; no movement is discernible, except for the distant decline of Third World growth rates. It represents the core of the empire's foreign economic policy: all markets are free, all countries are open, "do it *our* way." Around the core are the business lobby and the Washington insiders that instruct it. Then there are the institutions associated with open markets: the belief that the nationality of a firm's ownership doesn't matter; that labor can be hired and fired at will; that knowledge is free.

There, not far away but still too hot to touch, is the great ball of fire of the giants. Their policies continue to bounce around. They are experimenting with the elements, sampling the water, testing different markets, and picking up knowledge for whatever it's worth. At the center of the ball is the core of what giants have used to industrialize, some more successfully than others: they have relied on their manufacturing experience, education, and a working relationship between business and government to ensure that policies always shift and change as needs arise and external shocks occur. In the best giants, performance standards discipline subsidy recipients through a hybrid institutional structure. The market is there and grows more liberal, because "do it your way" has limits set by the World Bank, IMF, and WTO. But liberalization does not necessarily arrive out of any strong conviction. The eye of the storm is labor and income distribution, and the key to how well a giant succeeds is how well it creates skilled jobs and opportunities for highly trained managers and engineers. For the first time in modern history, great balls of fire illuminate the skyline.

The mature Second American Empire competes globally on the basis of *efficiency*, having already exploited its secret technology and proprietary brand name. Efficiency is what free markets are all about. By contrast, with its holes in the road, high unemployment, and income disparities (which are sometimes *less* than those of the empire!), the immature giant needs skills that will enable it to *learn* new technologies fast. In hand-me-down high-tech industries like calculators, computers, and cell phones, after millions of a product have already been sold and profit margins are diving, survival depends on how many units of a product a new entrant can produce. The giant thus needs project execution skills. It has to expand capacity at the drop of a hat in order to gain the volume that is a matter of survival. In mid-tech industries ranging from automobiles to steel, where low costs depend on huge capacity and thousands of experienced workers, competition from advanced countries is fierce. These industries are the backbone of an industrial society. Business and government in countries still catching up must join forces to counter the "dumping" of established firms, which send prices to the graveyard. A joint effort is needed until a brand name can be established and technology transfer is complete. Efficiency is still down the road; first come the big leaps needed to enter monopolistic markets.

Economic development thus has two approaches. One, which supposedly is applicable to rich and poor countries alike, recommends free markets to maximize efficiency. The greater efficiency is, the greater development is. The other, a less formal body of thought, likens development to learning technological capabilities and getting institutions to work, including markets—themselves an institution. The better the institutional system in place, the faster the development. To break the chains of static comparative advantage that for centuries bound them to mining minerals and manufacturing miniature dolls, developing countries must again be free to choose their own model.

If this argument is right, and if giants fan out to the earth's four corners, the world will again tip toward the learning mode. This will enable countries with *postwar* manufacturing experience—from Algeria and Egypt to South Africa and Peru—to resume raising their living standards.

American bureaucrats in Washington and business people in Palo Alto want to travel at the same speed as China and other giants. Keeping up requires discarding old baggage to be light and faster. The United States has to change its foreign economic policies and move altogether beyond the Second American Empire to succeed. The world's problems are becoming increasingly global, such as the earth's warming, and if they are to be solved, responsibility must be joint and power must be shared.

Notes

Chapter 1

1. This is the title of Goodwin's book on the Roosevelts: D. K. Goodwin, *No Ordinary Time: Franklin and Eleanor Roosevelt: The Home Front in World War II* (New York: Touchstone, 1994).

2. J. V. Puryear, *International Economics and Diplomacy in the Near East* (Stanford: Stanford University Press, 1935), 117.

3. United States Trade Representative, *Trade Policy Agenda and...Annual Report* (Washington, D.C.: Office of the United States Trade Representative, 1998), 11. The Trade Representative at this time was Charlene Barshevsky.

4. The idea of retained institutions is Joel Siegel's, Harvard Business School.

5. A. Solimano, ed., *Vanishing Growth in Latin America* (Northampton, Mass.: Edward Elgar, 2006), 3.

6. F. Levy, *New Dollars and Dreams* (New York: Russell Sage Foundation, 1998).

7. P. Krugman, "Graduates versus Oligarchs," *New York Times*, February 27, 2006.

8. For different types of data on equality, see publications by Rolph van der Hoeven at the International Labour Office, Geneva, and Giovanni Andrea Cornea, at the United Nations University/Wider, Helsinki.

9. J. A. Padin, "Puerto Rico in the Post War: Liberalized Development Banking and the Fall of the 'Fifth Tiger.'" *World Development* 31, no. 2 (2003), 281–301.

10. J. Forero, "Trade Proposal Splits Bolivian City," *New York Times*, March 9, 2004, C1.

11. R. L. Tignor, *Capitalism and Nationalism at the End of Empire: State and Business in Decolonizing Egypt, Nigeria, and Kenya, 1945–1963* (Princeton: Princeton University Press, 1998).

12. E. Gibbon, *The Portable Gibbon: The Decline and Fall of the Roman Empire* (New York: Viking, 1952); A. J. Toynbee, *A Study of History*, 12 vols. (London: Oxford University Press, 1934–1961).

13. J. Perlez, "China's Role Emerges as Major Issue for Southeast Asia," *New York Times*, March 14, 2006, A3.

14. H. Myint, *The Economics of the Developing Countries* (1964; reprint, New York: Praeger, 1995).

15. A. Hourani, *A History of the Arab Peoples* (Cambridge: Belknap Press of Harvard University Press, 1991).

16. United Nations, *Human Development Report 2002* (New York: Oxford University Press, 2002).

17. J. Diamond, *Guns, Germs, and Steel* (New York: Norton, 1997).

Chapter 2

1. Niall Ferguson has written two thoughtful and well-researched compliments to empire: N. Ferguson, *Empire: The Rise and Demise of the British World Order and the Lessons for Global Power* (New York: Basic Books, 2003), and N. Ferguson, *Colossus: The Rise and Fall of the American Empire* (New York: Penguin, 2004).

2. Silberner, quoted in P. K. O'Brien, *Power with Profit: The State and the Economy, 1688–1815*, Inaugural Lecture, University of London (London: University of London, 1991), 33.

3. D. R. Headrick, *The Tentacles of Progress: Technology Transfer in the Age of Imperialism, 1850–1940* (New York: Oxford University Press, 1988), 367.

4. Some of these examples are drawn from R. L. Tignor, *Capitalism and Nationalism at the End of Empire: State and Business in Decolonizing Egypt, Nigeria, and Kenya, 1945–1963* (Princeton: Princeton University Press, 1998).

5. P. K. O'Brien, "Intercontinental Trade and the Development of the Third World since the Industrial Revolution," *Journal of World History* 8, no. 1 (1997), 75–133.

6. U. S. Mehta, *Liberalism and Empire: A Study in Nineteenth-Century British Liberal Thought* (Chicago: University of Chicago Press, 1999), 7.

7. A. H. Amsden, *The Rise of "the Rest": Challenges to the West from Late-Industrializing Economies* (New York: Oxford University Press, 2001).

8. G. Tortella, ed., *Education and Economic Development since the Industrial Revolution* (Valencia: Generalitat Valenciana, 1990).

9. W. A. Lewis, *Tropical Development, 1880–1913* (Evanston, Ill.: Northwestern University Press, 1970), 214.

10. Ibid. Not all administrations used the old power structure to govern. In the Ivory Coast, for instance, "colonial officials were conscious that they were ruining an old class system. . . . Do not let us be afraid to sweep Africa clean of its feudalists by officializing them." J. Rapley, *Ivoirien Capitalism: African Entrepreneurs in Côte d'Ivoire* (Boulder, Colo.: Lynne Rienner, 1993), 27.

11. Headrick, *The Tentacles of Progress*, 367.

12. A. D. Chandler Jr., *The Visible Hand: The Managerial Revolution in American Business* (Cambridge: Harvard University Press, 1977), 87.

13. Headrick, *The Tentacles of Progress*, 82.

14. Ibid.

15. M. Wilkins, *The Maturing of Multinational Enterprise: American Business Abroad from 1914 to 1970* (Cambridge: Harvard University Press, 1974), 218–219, 227.

16. M. Rudner, *Malaysian Development: A Retrospective* (Ottawa: Carleton University Press, 1994), 157.

17. D. Banerjee, *Colonialism in Action* (Hyderabad: Orient Longman, 1999), 121.

18. This section and the next borrow from Amsden, *The Rise of "the Rest."*

19. Lewis, *Tropical Development*, 212.

20. T. J. Bassett, *The Peasant Cotton Revolution in West Africa: Côte d'Ivoire, 1880–1995* (Cambridge: Cambridge University Press, 2001), 58.

21. Ibid., 59.

22. Ibid.

23. H. Myint, *The Economics of the Developing Countries* (1964; New York: Praeger, 1995).

24. Quoted in C. Issawi, *The Fertile Crescent 1800–1914* (New York: Oxford University Press, 1988), 39.

25. R. Graham, *Britain and the Onset of Modernization in Brazil 1850–1914* (London: Cambridge University Press, 1968), 153.

26. D. K. Lieu, *The Growth and Industrialization of Shanghai* (Shanghai: China Institute of Pacific Relations, 1936), 34.

27. C. Geertz, *Peddlers and Princes: Social Development and Economic Change in Two Indonesian Towns* (Chicago: University of Chicago Press, 1963), 71.

28. D. Quataert, *Manufacturing and Technology Transfer in the Ottoman Empire, 1800–1914* (Istanbul and Strasbourg: Isis Press, 1992), 32.

29. Graham, *Britain and the Onset of Modernization in Brazil*, 153.

30. J. H. Coatsworth, *Growth against Development: The Economic Impact of Railroads in Porfirian Mexico* (DeKalb, Ill.: Northern Illinois University Press, 1981), 38.

31. D. M. Phelps, *Migration of Industry to South America* (New York: McGraw-Hill, 1936).

32. P. Shepherd, "Transnational Corporations and the Denationalisation of the Latin American Cigarette Industry," in A. Teichova, M. Levy-Leboyer, and H. Nussbaum, eds., *Historical Studies in International Corporate Business* (Cambridge: Cambridge University Press, 1989), 201–228.

33. J. C. Crossley and R. Greenhill, "The River Plate Beef Trade," in D. C. M. Platt, ed., *Business Imperialism, 1840–1930* (Oxford: Clarendon Press, 1977), 284–334.

34. P. H. Lewis, *The Crisis of Argentine Capitalism* (Chapel Hill: University of North Carolina Press, 1990), 51.

35. S. J. Koh, *Stages of Industrial Development in Asia: A Comparative History of the Cotton Industry in Japan, India, China, and Korea* (Philadelphia: University of Pennsylvania Press, 1966).

36. E. P. Reubens, "Foreign Capital and Domestic Development in Japan," in S. Kuznets, W. E. Moore, and J. J. Spengler, eds., *Economic Growth: Brazil, India, Japan* (Durham: Duke University Press, 1955), 179–228.

37. D. Tripathi and M. Mehta, *Business Houses in Western India: A Study of Entrepreneurial Responses, 1850–1956* (Columbia, Mo.: South Asia Publications, 1990), 61.

38. E. C. Clark, "The Emergence of Textile Manufacturing Entrepreneurs in Turkey, 1804–1968," Ph.D. diss., Princeton University, 1969.

39. C. Keyder, "Manufacturing in the Ottoman Empire and in Republican Turkey, ca. 1900–1950," in D. Quataert, ed., *Ottoman Industry in the Eighteenth Century: General Framework, Characteristics, and Main Trends* (Albany: State University of New York Press, 1994), 123–164.

40. C. K. Moser, *The Cotton Textile Industry of Far Eastern Countries* (Boston: Pepperell Manufacturing Co., 1930), 166.

41. S. Cochran, *Big Business in China: Sino-Foreign Rivalry in the Cigarette Industry, 1890–1930* (Cambridge: Harvard University Press, 1980), 74.

42. Clark, "The Emergence of Textile Manufacturing Entrepreneurs in Turkey."

43. S. Yonekura, *The Japanese Iron and Steel Industry, 1850–1990* (New York: St. Martin's, 1994), 44.

44. S. H. Haber, *Industry and Underdevelopment: The Industrialization of Mexico, 1890–1940* (Stanford: Stanford University Press, 1989), 5.

45. D. Keremitsis, *The Cotton Textile Industry in Porfiriato Mexico, 1870–1910* (New York: Garland Publishing, 1987), 197.

46. A. S. Pearse, *The Cotton Industry of Japan and China* (Manchester, U.K.: International Federation of Cotton and Allied Textile Industries, 1929).

47. K. Chao, "The Growth of a Modern Textile Industry and the Competition with Handicrafts," in D. H. Perkins, ed., *China's Modern Economy in Historical Perspective* (Stanford: Stanford University Press, 1975), 167–202.

48. Quoted in Graham, *Britain and the Onset of Modernization in Brazil*, 139.

49. T. Chokki, "Labor Management in the Cotton Spinning Industry," in N. Keiichiro, ed., *Labor and Management: Proceedings of the Fourth Fuji Conference* (Tokyo: University of Tokyo Press, 1979), 149.

50. L. C. A. Knowles, *The Economic Development of the British Overseas Empire* (London: George Routledge, 1928), 231.

51. R. H. Myers and Y. Saburo, "Agricultural Development in the Empire," in R. H. Myers and M. R. Peattie, eds., *The Japanese Colonial Empire, 1895–1945* (Princeton: Princeton University Press, 1984), 420–452.

52. Cited in P. Robb, "Bihar, the Colonial State and Agricultural Development in India, 1880–1920," *Indian Economic and Social History Review* 25, no. 2 (1988), 224.

53. Knowles, *The Economic Development of the British Overseas Empire*, 224.

54. Headrick, *The Tentacles of Progress*.

55. See note 2, this chapter.

Chapter 3

1. C. Thorne, *The Issue of War: States, Societies, and the Far Eastern Conflict of 1941–1945* (New York: Oxford University Press, 1985), 184.

2. Ibid.

3. J. Goldstein and R. O. Keohane, eds., *Ideas and Foreign Policy* (Ithaca: Cornell University Press, 1993), 24.

4. V. Bulmer-Thomas, *The Economic History of Latin America since Independence* (Cambridge: Cambridge University Press, 1994), 257.

5. D. Kapur, J. P. Lewis, et al., eds., *The World Bank: Its First Half Century* (Washington, D.C.: Brookings, 1997).

6. J. Gallagher and R. Robinson, "The Imperialism of Free Trade," *Economic History Review* 6, no. 1 (1953), 1–15.

7. Cited in A. E. J. Eckes, *Opening America's Market: U.S. Foreign Trade Policy since 1776* (Chapel Hill: University of North Carolina Press, 1995), 141.

8. D. Acheson, *Present at the Creation: My Years in the State Department* (New York: Norton, 1969), 9.

9. Quoted in R. Skidelsky, *John Maynard Keynes: Fighting for Freedom, 1937–1946* (New York: Penguin, 2000), 179.

10. J. M. Dobson, *Two Centuries of Tariffs: The Background and Emergence of the U.S. International Trade Commission* (Washington, D.C.: United States International Trade Commission, U.S. Government Printing Office, 1976).

11. Eckes, *Opening America's Market*, xix. Quotations and information on trade and tariffs in this and following paragraphs are from this book unless otherwise noted.

12. C. K. Harley, "International Competitiveness of the Antebellum American Cotton Textile Industry," *Journal of Economic History* 52, no. 3 (1992), 559–584. The United States could not compete without tariffs.

13. P. Low, *Trading Free: The GATT and U.S. Trade Policy* (New York: Twentieth Century Fund Press, 1993), 26.

14. Information on GATT negotiations is from Eckes, *Opening America's Market*.

15. Low, *Trading Free*, 244.

Chapter 4

1. K. Raffer and H. W. Singer, *The Foreign Aid Business: Economic Assistance and Development Co-operation* (Cheltenham, U.K.: Edward Elgar, 1996). Information in the next paragraph is also from this source.

2. A. H. Amsden, *The Rise of "the Rest": Challenges to the West from Late-Industrializing Economies* (New York: Oxford University Press, 2001).

3. L. B. Pearson, *Partners in Development* (the "Pearson Report") (New York: Praeger, 1969), 173.

4. Raffer and Singer, *The Foreign Aid Business*.

5. R. S. Anderson, E. Levy, et al., *Rice Science and Development Politics* (Oxford: Clarendon Press, 1991). Quotations and information on the Green Revolution in this and following paragraphs are from this book unless otherwise noted. See also B. H. Farmer, ed., *Green Revolution? Technology and Change in Rice-Growing Areas of Tamil Nadu and Sri Lanka* (Boulder, Colo.: Westview Press, 1977).

6. World Bank, *World Development Report, Poverty* (Washington, D.C.: World Bank, 1990), 82.

7. M. T. Klare and C. Arnson, "Exporting Recession," in R. Fagen, ed., *Capitalism and the State in US-Latin American Relations* (Stanford: Stanford University Press, 1979), 142. Other information in this and following paragraphs related to Latin American defense are from this source, unless otherwise noted.

8. F. K. McCann Jr., *The Brazilian-American Alliance, 1937–1945* (Princeton: Princeton University Press, 1973), 457.

9. Klare and Arnson, "Exporting Recession," 149.

10. T. Hikino, "Economic Theories and Japanese Economic Development after World War II," *Kyoto Economic Journal* (Winter 2004), 36–38.

11. S. P. Huntington, *Political Order in Changing Societies* (New Haven: Yale University Press, 1968).

Chapter 5

1. Hao, Y.-P., *The Comprador in Nineteenth Century China: Bridge between East and West* (Cambridge: Harvard University Press, 1970).

2. A. H. Amsden, *The Rise of "the Rest": Challenges to the West from Late-Industrializing Economies* (New York: Oxford University Press, 2001).

3. L. B. Pearson, *Partners in Development* (New York: Praeger, 1969).

4. A. Maizels, "Economic Dependence on Commodities," in Y. Toye, ed., *Trade and Development: Directions for the 21st Century* (Cheltenham, U.K.: Edward Elgar, 2003).

Chapter 6

1. World Bank, *The East Asian Miracle: Economic Growth and Public Policy* (New York: Oxford University Press, 1993), 5.

2. Japan used two rules to pick winners: the growth rate of output, and the growth rate of productivity (both worldwide). A. H. Amsden and K. Suzumura, "An Interview with Miyohei Shinohara: Nonconformism in Japanese Economic Thought," *Journal of the Japanese and International Economies* 15 (2001).

3. Banco Nacional de Desenvolvimento Econômico e Social, *BNDES, 40 Years: An Agent of Change* (Rio de Janeiro: BNDES, 1992), 9, 18–19.

4. Cited by R. Wade, *Governing the Market: Economic Theory and the Role of the Government in East Asian Industrialization* (Princeton: Princeton University Press, 1990), 87.

5. T. Patcharee, "Patterns of Industrial Policymaking in Thailand: Japanese Multinationals and Domestic Actors in the Automobile and Electrical Appliances Industries," Ph.D. diss., University of Wisconsin, 1985.

6. Türkiye Is Bankasi A.S., *Development Plan of Turkey, Second Five-Year (1968–1972)* (Ankara: Economic Research Department, Türkiye Is Bankasi A.S., 1967), 45.

7. Nacional Financiera, S.A., *Informe annual* (Mexico, D.F.: Nacional Financiera, S.A., various years).

8. Korea Development Bank, *Annual Report* (Seoul: Korea Development Bank, various years).

9. M. Shinohara, *Industrial Growth, Trade, and Dynamic Patterns in the Japanese Economy* (Tokyo: University of Tokyo Press, 1982), 144.

10. On Brazil and Mexico, see P. Krugman, "Import Protection as Export Promotion: International Competition in the Presence of Oligopoly and Economies of Scale," in H. Kierzkowski, ed., *Monopolistic Competition and International Trade* (New York: Oxford University Press, 1984).

11. R. Ffrench-Davis, P. Leiva, et al., *Trade Liberalization in Chile: Experiences and Prospects* (Geneva: United Nations Conference on Trade and Development, 1992), 97.

12. Y. Lim, "Public Policy for Upgrading Industrial Technology in Korea" (Massachusetts Institute of Technology, 1999), 146.

13. A. H. Amsden, *Asia's Next Giant: South Korea and Late Industrialization* (New York: Oxford University Press, 1989).

14. W.-w. Chu, "The Effect of Globalization and Democratization on Taiwan's Industrial Policy," Academia Sinica, Institute for Social Science Policy, Taipei, 1998, 16. See also A. H. Amsden and W.-w. Chu, *Beyond Late Development: Taiwan's Upgrading Policies* (Cambridge: MIT Press, 2003).

15. T. Baysan and C. Blitzer, "Turkey's Trade Liberalization in the 1980s and Prospects for Its Sustainability," in T. Aricanli and D. Rodrik, eds., *The Political Economy of Turkey: Debt, Adjustment and Sustainability* (Basingstoke, U.K.: Macmillan, 1990), 9–36.

16. See R. McGregor, "The World Begins at Home for TCL," *Financial Times*, November 6, 2001, 23.

17. A. H. Amsden, *The Rise of "the Rest": Challenges to the West from Late-Industrializing Economies* (New York: Oxford University Press, 2001).

18. Ibid.

19. Ibid.

20. L. Kim, *Imitation to Innovation: The Dynamics of Korea's Technological Learning* (Boston: Harvard Business School Press, 1997).

21. Y. Sato, "Diverging Development Paths of the Electronics Industry in Korea and Taiwan," *Developing Economies* 35, no. 4 (1997), 401–421.

22. G. San, "An Overview of Policy Priorities for Industrial Development in Taiwan," *Journal of Industry Studies* 2, no. 1 (1995), 27–55.

23. Amsden, *The Rise of "the Rest."*

24. H. Poot, A. Kuyvenhoven, et al., *Industrialisation and Trade in Indonesia* (Yogyakarta: Gadjah Mada University Press, 1990).

25. F. Senses, "An Assessment of the Pattern of Turkish Manufactured Export Growth in the 1980s and Its Prospects," in Aricanli and Rodrik, eds., *The Political Economy of Turkey*, 60–77; Baysan and Blitzer, "Turkey's Trade Liberalization in the 1980s."

26. J. M. Máttar, "La competitividad de la industria química," in F. Clavijo and J. I. Casar, eds., *La industria mexicana en el mercado mundial: Elementos para una política industrial* (Mexico, D.F.: Fondo de Cultura Económica, 1994), 159–312.

27. H. Shapiro, *Engines of Growth: The State and Transnational Auto Companies in Brazil* (Cambridge: Cambridge University Press, 1994).

28. E. Sridharan, *The Political Economy of Industrial Promotion: Indian, Brazilian, and Korean Electronics in Comparative Perspective, 1969–1994* (Westport, Conn.: Praeger, 1996).

29. Korea Development Bank, *Annual Report* (various years).

30. Amsden, *The Rise of "the Rest."*

31. I. M. Salleh and S. D. Meyananthan, "Malaysia: Growth, Equity, and Structural Transformation," in D. M. Leipziger, ed., *Lessons from East Asia* (Ann Arbor: University of Michigan Press, 1997), 279–343.

32. C. P. Blair, "Nacional Financiera: Entrepreneurship in a Mixed Economy," in R. Vernon, ed., *Public Policy and Private Enterprise in Mexico* (Cambridge: Harvard University Press, 1964), 191–240; E. J. Willis, *The Politicized Bureaucracy: Regimes, Presidents and Economic Policy in Brazil* (Boston: Boston College, 1990); and P. F. Oreffice and G. R. Baker, "The Development of a Joint Petrochemical Venture in Chile—The Petrodow Project," in N. Beredjick, ed., *Problems and Prospects of the Chemical Industries in the Less Developed Countries: Case Histories* (New York: American Chemical Society, 1970), 122–129.

Chapter 7

1. D. Hirst, *Oil and Public Opinion in the Middle East* (New York: Praeger, 1966).

2. Cited in A. Sampson, *The Seven Sisters: The Great Oil Companies and the World They Made* (London: Hodder and Stoughton, 1975), 216.

3. Quoted in N. Sheehan, *A Bright Shining Lie: John Paul Vann and America in Vietnam* (New York: Random House, 1988), 147. Information on Vietnam is drawn from this source and from G. M. Kahin, *Intervention: How America Became Involved in Vietnam* (New York: Doubleday, Anchor, 1987), and various readings in M. E. Gettleman, J. Franklin, et al., eds., *Vietnam and America: A Documented History*, rev. ed. (New York: Grove Press, 1995).

4. N. V. Long, "Vietnam's Revolutionary Tradition," in Gettleman et al., *Vietnam and America*, 11.

5. The material on Ho Chi Minh in this and the following two paragraphs is drawn from Sheehan, *A Bright Shining Lie*, 146–147.

6. See Kahin, *Intervention*, 103.

7. V. N. Giap, "Vietnamese Victory: Dien Bien Phu, 1954," in Gettleman et al., *Vietnam and America.*

8. D. D. Eisenhower, *Mandate for Change, 1953–1956: The White House Years* (Garden City, N.Y.: Doubleday, 1963), 337–338.

9. A. H. Amsden, *Asia's Next Giant: South Korea and Late Industrialization* (New York: Oxford University Press, 1989), 305.

10. Kahin, *Intervention*, 27.

11. D. Wurfel, *Filipino Politics: Development and Decay* (Ithaca: Cornell University Press, 1988), 25.

12. Sheehan, *A Bright Shining Lie*, 144.

13. Sampson, *The Seven Sisters.*

14. F. Fitzgerald, "Giving the Shah Everything He Wants," *Harper's*, November 1974.

15. This and other citations on the Suez Canal are from R. L. Tignor, *Capitalism and Nationalism at the End of Empire: State and Business in Decolonizing Egypt, Nigeria, and Kenya, 1945–1963* (Princeton: Princeton University Press, 1998).

16. W. R. Neikirk, *Volcker: Portrait of the Money Man* (New York: Congdon & Weed, 1987).

Chapter 8

1. B. Eichengreen, *Globalizing Capital* (Princeton: Princeton University Press, 1996), 94.

2. W. R. Neikirk, *Volcker: Portrait of the Money Man* (New York: Congdon & Weed, 1987), 176. Other material on Volcker is from the same source unless otherwise indicated.

3. Ibid.

4. E. Kiray, "Turkish Debt and Conditionality in Historical Perspective: A Comparison of the 1980s with the 1860s," in T. Aricanli and D. Rodrik, eds., *The Political Economy of Turkey: Debt, Adjustment and Sustainability* (Basingstoke, U.K.: Macmillan, 1990), 254–268.

5. R. I. McKinnon, "Currency Wars," *Wall Street Journal*, July 29, 2005.

6. My discussion with Paul Volcker, Reuter's Forum, Faculty Club, Columbia University, March 8, 2003.

7. *New York Times*, January 21, 2005.

8. M. M. Moreira, *Estrangeiros em uma economia aberta: Impactos recentes sobre productividade, concentração e comércio exterior* (Rio de Janeiro: Banco Nacional de Desenvolvimento Econômico e Social, 1999).

9. A. K. Cairncross, *Factors in Economic Development* (New York: Praeger, 1962).

10. E. P. Reubens, "Foreign Capital and Domestic Development in Japan," in S. Kuznets, W. E. Moore, and J. J. Spengler, eds., *Economic Growth: Brazil, India, Japan* (Durham: Duke University Press, 1955), 179–228.

11. This and the following figures are drawn from the United Nations *World Investment Report* (Geneva: United Nations, various years).

Chapter 9

1. D. Kapur, J. P. Lewis, et al., eds., *The World Bank: Its First Half Century* (Washington, D.C.: Brookings, 1997), 1194.

2. Ibid., 22, 339, 511, 1193.

3. E. Berg, quoted in P. Mosley, J. Harrigan, et al., *Aid and Power: The World Bank and Policy-Based Lending in the 1980s* (London: Routledge, 1991), 24.

4. S. A. Zaidi, *Issues in Pakistan's Economy* (Oxford: Oxford University Press, 1999), 315.

5. P. Blustein, "World Bank Chief to Leave Position Later This Year," *Asian Wall Street Journal*, January 4, 2005, A8.

6. A. Sen, *Development as Freedom* (New York: Anchor, 2000), 4.

7. C. Adelman, "A High Quality of Mercy" (op ed piece), *New York Times*, January 4, 2005.

8. S. M. Rutnagur, *Bombay Industries: The Cotton Mills* (Bombay: Indian Textile Journal, 1927), 50–51.

9. R. MacMullen, *Corruption and the Decline of Rome* (New Haven: Yale University Press, 1988).

10. F. Jawara and A. Kwa, *Behind the Scenes at the WTO: The Real World of International Trade Negotiations* (London: Zed, 2003), 301.

11. D. Nayyar, "An Analysis of the Stagnation in India's Cotton Textile Exports during the 1960s," *Oxford Bulletin of Economics and Statistics* 35, no. 1 (1973), 1–19.

12. B. Kosacoff, *Corporate Strategies under Structural Adjustment in Argentina* (Basingstoke, U.K.: Macmillan, 2000).

Chapter 10

1. Data may be found in A. H. Amsden, *The Rise of "the Rest": Challenges to the West from Late-Industrializing Economies* (New York: Oxford University Press, 2001).

2. A. H. Amsden and L. Kim, "A Comparative Analysis of Local and Transnational Corporations in the Korean Automobile Industry," in D.-K. Kim and L. Kim, eds., *Management behind Industrialization: Readings in Korean Business* (Seoul: Korea University Press, 1985), 579–596.

Chapter 11

1. K. Kojima, "Asian Economic Integration for the 21st Century," *East Asian Economic Perspectives* 13 (March 2002), 1–38.

2. The metaphor is from Sidney Pollard, one of Europe's greatest economic historians.

3. J. Perlez, "China's Role Emerges as Major Issue for Southeast Asia," *New York Times*, March 14, 2006, A3; emphasis added.

4. United Nations Conference on Trade and Development, *Yearbook of Trade and Development Statistics* (Geneva: United Nations Conference on Trade and Development, various years).

5. Kojima, "Asian Economic Integration for the 21st Century."

6. Manmohan Singh, speech to Asia Society conference, Mumbai, March 18, 2006.

7. Singapore *Straits Times*, March 2005.

Bibliography

Acheson, D. (1969). *Present at the Creation: My Years in the State Department.* New York: Norton.

Adelman, C. (2005). "A High Quality of Mercy." *New York Times,* January 4.

Agosin, M. R., and D. Tussie (1993). *Trade and Growth: New Dilemmas in Trade Policy.* London: St. Martin's Press.

Amsden, A. H. (1989). *Asia's Next Giant: South Korea and Late Industrialization.* New York: Oxford University Press.

Amsden, A. H. (2001). *The Rise of "the Rest": Challenges to the West from Late-Industrializing Economies.* New York: Oxford University Press.

Amsden, A. H., and W.-w. Chu (2003). *Beyond Late Development: Taiwan's Upgrading Policies.* Cambridge: MIT Press.

Amsden, A. H., and L. Kim (1985). "A Comparative Analysis of Local and Transnational Corporations in the Korean Automobile Industry." In D.-K. Kim and L. Kim, eds., *Management behind Industrialization: Readings in Korean Business.* Seoul: Korea University Press, 579–596.

Amsden, A. H., and K. Suzumura (2001). "An Interview with Miyohei Shinohara: Nonconformism in Japanese Economic Thought." *Journal of the Japanese and International Economies* 15.

Anderson, R. S., E. Levy, et al. (1991). *Rice Science and Development Politics.* Oxford: Clarendon Press.

Baldwin, D. A. (1966). *Economic Development and American Foreign Policy, 1943–62.* Chicago: University of Chicago Press.

Banco Nacional de Desenvolvimento Econômico e Social (1992). *BNDES, 40 Years: An Agent of Change.* Rio de Janeiro: BNDES.

Banerjee, D. (1999). *Colonialism in Action.* Hyderabad: Orient Longman.

Bassett, T. J. (2001). *The Peasant Cotton Revolution in West Africa: Côte d'Ivoire, 1880–1995*. Cambridge: Cambridge University Press.

Baysan, T., and C. Blitzer (1990). "Turkey's Trade Liberalization in the 1980s and Prospects for Its Sustainability." In T. Aricanli and D. Rodrik, eds., *The Political Economy of Turkey: Debt, Adjustment and Sustainability*. Basingstoke, U.K.: Macmillan, 9–36.

Becker, E. (2004). "October Trade Gap a Record: Up 9 percent in Month." *New York Times*, December 14, C4.

Blair, C. P. (1964). "Nacional Financiera: Entrepreneurship in a Mixed Economy." In R. Vernon, ed., *Public Policy and Private Enterprise in Mexico*. Cambridge: Harvard University Press, 191–240.

Blustein, P. (2005). "World Bank Chief to Leave Position Later This Year." *Asian Wall Street Journal*, January 4, A8.

Bulmer-Thomas, V. (1994). *The Economic History of Latin America since Independence*. Cambridge: Cambridge University Press.

Cairncross, A. K. (1962). *Factors in Economic Development*. New York: Praeger.

Chandler, A. D., Jr. (1977). *The Visible Hand: The Managerial Revolution in American Business*. Cambridge: Harvard University Press.

Chao, K. (1975). "The Growth of a Modern Textile Industry and the Competition with Handicrafts." In D. H. Perkins, ed., *China's Modern Economy in Historical Perspective*. Stanford: Stanford University Press, 167–202.

Chokki, T. (1979). "Labor Management in the Cotton Spinning Industry." In N. Keiichiro, ed., *Labor and Management: Proceedings of the Fourth Fuji Conference*. Tokyo: University of Tokyo Press.

Chu, W.-w. (1998). "The Effect of Globalization and Democratization on Taiwan's Industrial Policy." Academia Sinica, Institute for Social Science Policy, Taipei.

Clark, E. C. (1969). "The Emergence of Textile Manufacturing Entrepreneurs in Turkey, 1804–1968." Ph.D. diss., Princeton University.

Coatsworth, J. H. (1981). *Growth against Development: The Economic Impact of Railroads in Porfirian Mexico*. DeKalb, Ill.: Northern Illinois University Press.

Cochran, S. (1980). *Big Business in China: Sino-Foreign Rivalry in the Cigarette Industry, 1890–1930*. Cambridge: Harvard University Press.

Crossley, J. C., and R. Greenhill (1977). "The River Plate Beef Trade." In D. C. M. Platt, ed., *Business Imperialism, 1840–1930*. Oxford: Clarendon Press, 284–334.

Diamond, J. (1997). *Guns, Germs, and Steel: The Fates of Human Societies*. New York: Norton.

Dobson, J. M. (1976). *Two Centuries of Tariffs: The Background and Emergence of the U.S. International Trade Commission.* Washington, D.C.: United States International Trade Commission, U.S. Government Printing Office.

Dower, J. W. (1999). *Embracing Defeat: Japan in the Wake of World War II.* New York: Norton.

Eckes, A. E. J. (1995). *Opening America's Market: U.S. Foreign Trade Policy since 1776.* Chapel Hill: University of North Carolina Press.

Eichengreen, B. (1996). *Globalizing Capital.* Princeton: Princeton University Press.

Eisenhower, D. D. (1963). *Mandate for Change, 1953–1956: The White House Years.* Garden City, N.Y.: Doubleday.

Farmer, B. H., ed. (1977). *Green Revolution? Technology and Change in Rice-Growing Areas of Tamil Nadu and Sri Lanka.* Boulder, Colo.: Westview Press.

Ferguson, N. (2003). *Empire: The Rise and Demise of the British World Order and the Lessons for Global Power.* New York: Basic Books.

Ferguson, N. (2004). *Colossus: The Rise and Fall of the American Empire.* New York: Penguin.

Ffrench-Davis, R., P. Leiva, et al. (1992). *Trade Liberalization in Chile: Experiences and Prospects.* Geneva: United Nations Conference on Trade and Development.

Fitzgerald, F. (1974). "Giving the Shah Everything He Wants." *Harper's*, November.

Forero, J. (2004). "Trade Proposal Splits Bolivian City." *New York Times*, March 9, C1.

Gallagher, J., and R. Robinson (1953). "The Imperialism of Free Trade." *Economic History Review* 6, no. 1, 1–15.

Geertz, C. (1963). *Peddlers and Princes: Social Development and Economic Change in Two Indonesian Towns.* Chicago: University of Chicago Press.

Gettleman, M. E., J. Franklin, et al., eds. (1995). *Vietnam and America: A Documented History*, rev ed. New York: Grove Press.

Gibbon, E. (1952). *The Portable Gibbon: The Decline and Fall of the Roman Empire.* New York: Viking.

Goldstein, J., and R. O. Keohane, eds. (1993). *Ideas and Foreign Policy: Beliefs, Institutions, and Political Change.* Ithaca: Cornell University Press.

Goodwin, D. K. (1994). *No Ordinary Time: Franklin and Eleanor Roosevelt: The Home Front in World War II.* New York: Touchstone.

Graham, R. (1968). *Britain and the Onset of Modernization in Brazil 1850–1914.* London: Cambridge University Press.

Haber, S. H. (1989). *Industry and Underdevelopment: The Industrialization of Mexico, 1890–1940*. Stanford: Stanford University Press.

Hao, Y.-P. (1970). *The Comprador in Nineteenth Century China: Bridge between East and West*. Cambridge: Harvard University Press.

Harley, C. K. (1992). "International Competitiveness of the Antebellum American Cotton Textile Industry." *Journal of Economic History* 52, no. 3, 559–584.

Headrick, D. R. (1988). *The Tentacles of Progress: Technology Transfer in the Age of Imperialism, 1850–1940*. New York: Oxford University Press.

Hikino, T. (2004). "Economic Theories and Japanese Economic Development after World War II." *Kyoto Economic Journal* (Winter).

Hirst, D. (1966). *Oil and Public Opinion in the Middle East*. New York: Praeger.

Hochschield, A. (2005). "In the Heart of Darkness." *New York Review of Books*, October 6, 39–41.

Hourani, A. (1991). *A History of the Arab Peoples*. Cambridge: Belknap Press of Harvard University Press.

Huntington, S. P. (1968). *Political Order in Changing Societies*. New Haven: Yale University Press.

Issawi, C. (1988). *The Fertile Crescent 1800–1914*. New York: Oxford University Press.

Jawara, F., and A. Kwa (2003). *Behind the Scenes at the WTO: The Real World of International Trade Negotiations*. London: Zed.

Kahin, G. M. (1987). *Intervention: How America Became Involved in Vietnam*. New York: Doubleday, Anchor.

Kapur, D., J. P. Lewis, et al., eds. (1997). *The World Bank: Its First Half Century*. Washington, D.C.: Brookings.

Keremitsis, D. (1987). *The Cotton Textile Industry in Porfiriato Mexico, 1870–1910*. New York: Garland Publishing.

Keyder, C. (1994). "Manufacturing in the Ottoman Empire and in Republican Turkey, ca. 1900–1950." In D. Quataert, ed., *Ottoman Industry in the Eighteenth Century: General Framework, Characteristics, and Main Trends*. Albany: State University of New York Press, 123–164.

Khalaf, R. (2003). "Zoellick Criticism Sets Back Egypt Hopes on Free Trade Deal." *Wall Street Journal*, June 24.

Kim, L. (1997). *Imitation to Innovation: The Dynamics of Korea's Technological Learning*. Boston: Harvard Business School Press.

Kiray, E. (1990). "Turkish Debt and Conditionality in Historical Perspective: A Comparison of the 1980s with the 1860s." In T. Aricanli and D. Rodrik, eds., *The Political Economy of Turkey: Debt, Adjustment and Sustainability*. Basingstoke, U.K.: Macmillan, 254–268.

Klare, M. T., and C. Arnson (1979). "Exporting Recession." In R. Fagen, ed., *Capitalism and the State in US-Latin American Relations*. Stanford: Stanford University Press.

Knowles, L. C. A. (1928). *The Economic Development of the British Overseas Empire*. London: George Routledge.

Koh, S. J. (1966). *Stages of Industrial Development in Asia: A Comparative History of the Cotton Industry in Japan, India, China, and Korea*. Philadelphia: University of Pennsylvania Press.

Kojima, K. (2002). "Asian Economic Integration for the 21st Century." *East Asian Economic Perspectives* 13 (March), 1–38.

Korea Development Bank (various years). *Annual Report*. Seoul: Korea Development Bank.

Kosacoff, B. (2000). *Corporate Strategies under Structural Adjustment in Argentina*. Basingstoke, U.K.: Macmillan.

Krugman, P. (1984). "Import Protection as Export Promotion: International Competition in the Presence of Oligopoly and Economies of Scale." In H. Kierzkowski, ed., *Monopolistic Competition and International Trade*. New York: Oxford University Press.

Krugman, P. (2006). "Graduates versus Oligarchs." *New York Times*, February 27.

Lall, S. (1987). *Learning to Industrialize: The Acquisition of Technological Capability by India*. Basingstoke, U.K.: Macmillan.

Levy, F. (1998). *New Dollars and Dreams*. New York: Russell Sage Foundation.

Lewis, P. H. (1990). *The Crisis of Argentine Capitalism*. Chapel Hill: University of North Carolina Press.

Lewis, W. A. (1970). *Tropical Development, 1880–1913*. Evanston, Ill.: Northwestern University Press.

Lieu, D. K. (1936). *The Growth and Industrialization of Shanghai*. Shanghai: China Institute of Pacific Relations.

Lim, Y. (1999). *Public Policy for Upgrading Industrial Technology in Korea*. Massachusetts Institute of Technology.

Low, P. (1993). *Trading Free: The GATT and U.S. Trade Policy*. New York: Twentieth Century Fund Press.

MacMullen, R. (1988). *Corruption and the Decline of Rome*. New Haven: Yale University Press.

Maizels, A. (2003). "Economic Dependence on Commodities." In J. Toye, ed., *Trade and Development: Directions for the 21st Century*. Cheltenham, U.K.: Edward Elgar.

Máttar, J. M. (1994). "La competitividad de la industria química." In F. Clavijo and J. I. Casar, eds., *La industria mexicana en el mercado mundial: Elementos para una política industrial*. Mexico, D.F.: Fondo de Cultura Económica, 159–312.

McCann, F. K., Jr. (1973). *The Brazilian-American Alliance, 1937–1945*. Princeton: Princeton University Press.

McCullough, D. (1992). *Truman*. New York: Touchstone.

McGregor, R. (2001). "The World Begins at Home for TCL." *Financial Times*, November 6, 23.

McKinnon, R. I. (2005). "Currency Wars." *Wall Street Journal*, July 29.

Mehta, U. S. (1999). *Liberalism and Empire: A Study in Nineteenth-Century British Liberal Thought*. Chicago: University of Chicago Press.

Moreira, M. M. (1999). *Estrangeiros em uma economia aberta: Impactos recentes sobre productividade, concentração e comércio exterior*. Rio de Janeiro: Banco Nacional de Desenvolvimento Econômico e Social.

Moser, C. K. (1930). *The Cotton Textile Industry of Far Eastern Countries*. Boston: Pepperell Manufacturing Co.

Mosley, P., J. Harrigan, et al. (1991). *Aid and Power: The World Bank and Policy-Based Lending in the 1980s*. London: Routledge.

Myers, R. H., and Y. Saburo (1984). "Agricultural Development in the Empire." In R. H. Myers and M. R. Peattie, eds., *The Japanese Colonial Empire, 1895–1945*. Princeton: Princeton University Press, 420–452.

Myint, H. (1995). *The Economics of the Developing Countries*. New York: Praeger.

Nacional Financiera, S.A. (various years). *Informe annual*. Mexico, D.F.: Nacional Financiera, S.A.

Nayyar, D. (1973). "An Analysis of the Stagnation in India's Cotton Textile Exports during the 1960s." *Oxford Bulletin of Economics and Statistics* 35, no. 1, 1–19.

Neikirk, W. R. (1987). *Volcker: Portrait of the Money Man*. New York: Congdon & Weed.

Norman, E. H. (1940). *Japan's Emergence as a Modern State*. New York: Institute of Pacific Relations.

O'Brien, P. K. (1991). *Power with Profit: The State and the Economy, 1688–1815*. London: University of London.

O'Brien, P. K. (1997). "Intercontinental Trade and the Development of the Third World since the Industrial Revolution." *Journal of World History* 8, no. 1, 75–133.

Oreffice, P. F., and G. R. Baker (1970). "The Development of a Joint Petrochemical Venture in Chile—The Petrodow Project." In N. Beredjick, ed., *Problems and Prospects of the Chemical Industries in the Less Developed Countries: Case Histories*. New York: American Chemical Society, 122–129.

Organization for Economic Co-operation and Development (1994). *The New World Trading System: Readings*. OECD Documents. Paris: OECD.

Padin, J. A. (2003). "Puerto Rico in the Post War: Liberalized Development Banking and the Fall of the 'Fifth Tiger.'" *World Development* 31, no. 2, 281–301.

Park, S.-W. (1999). *Colonial Industrialization and Labor in Korea: The Onoda Cement Factory*. Cambridge: Harvard University Press.

Patcharee, T. (1985). "Patterns of Industrial Policymaking in Thailand: Japanese Multinationals and Domestic Actors in the Automobile and Electrical Appliances Industries." Ph.D. diss., University of Wisconsin.

Pearse, A. S. (1929). *The Cotton Industry of Japan and China*. Manchester, U.K.: International Federation of Cotton and Allied Textile Industries.

Pearson, L. B. (1969). *Partners in Development*. New York: Praeger.

Perlez, J. (2006). "China's Role Emerges as Major Issue for Southeast Asia." *New York Times*, March 14, A3.

Phelps, D. M. (1936). *Migration of Industry to South America*. New York: McGraw-Hill.

Poot, H., A. Kuyvenhoven, et al. (1990). *Industrialisation and Trade in Indonesia*. Yogyakarta: Gadjah Mada University Press.

Puryear, J. V. (1935). *International Economics and Diplomacy in the Near East*. Stanford: Stanford University Press.

Quataert, D. (1992). *Manufacturing and Technology Transfer in the Ottoman Empire, 1800–1914*. Istanbul and Strasbourg: Isis Press.

Raffer, K., and H. W. Singer (1996). *The Foreign Aid Business: Economic Assistance and Development Co-operation*. Cheltenham, U.K.: Edward Elgar.

Rapley, J. (1993). *Ivoirien Capitalism: African Entrepreneurs in Côte d'Ivoire*. Boulder, Colo.: Lynne Rienner.

Reubens, E. P. (1955). "Foreign Capital and Domestic Development in Japan." In S. Kuznets, W. E. Moore, and J. J. Spengler, eds., *Economic Growth: Brazil, India, Japan*. Durham: Duke University Press, 179–228.

Rhee, Y. (2004). "East Asian Monetary Integration: Destined to Fail?" *Social Science Japan Journal* 7, no. 1, 83–102.

Robb, P. (1988). "Bihar, the Colonial State and Agricultural Development in India, 1880–1920." *Indian Economic and Social History Review* 25, no. 2.

Rudner, M. (1994). *Malaysian Development: A Retrospective*. Ottawa: Carleton University Press.

Rutnagur, S. M. (1927). *Bombay Industries: The Cotton Mills*. Bombay: Indian Textile Journal.

Salleh, I. M., and S. D. Meyananthan (1997). "Malaysia: Growth, Equity, and Structural Transformation." In D. M. Leipziger, ed., *Lessons from East Asia*. Ann Arbor: University of Michigan Press, 279–343.

Sampson, A. (1975). *The Seven Sisters: The Great Oil Companies and the World They Made*. London: Hodder and Stoughton.

San, G. (1995). "An Overview of Policy Priorities for Industrial Development in Taiwan." *Journal of Industry Studies* 2, no. 1, 27.

Sato, Y. (1997). "Diverging Development Paths of the Electronics Industry in Korea and Taiwan." *Developing Economies* 35, no. 4, 401–421.

Sen, A. (2000). *Development as Freedom*. New York: Anchor.

Senses, F. (1990). "An Assessment of the Pattern of Turkish Manufactured Export Growth in the 1980s and Its Prospects." In T. Aricanli and D. Rodrik, eds., *The Political Economy of Turkey: Debt, Adjustment and Sustainability*. Basingstoke, U.K.: Macmillan, 60–77.

Shapiro, H. (1994). *Engines of Growth: The State and Transnational Auto Companies in Brazil*. Cambridge: Cambridge University Press.

Sheehan, N. (1988). *A Bright Shining Lie: John Paul Vann and America in Vietnam*. New York: Random House.

Shepherd, P. (1989). "Transnational Corporations and the Denationalisation of the Latin American Cigarette Industry." In A. Teichova, M. Levy-Leboyer, and H. Nussbaum, eds., *Historical Studies in International Corporate Business*. Cambridge: Cambridge University Press, 201–228.

Shinohara, M. (1982). *Industrial Growth, Trade, and Dynamic Patterns in the Japanese Economy*. Tokyo: University of Tokyo Press.

Silberner, E. (1972). *The Problem of War in Nineteenth Century Economic Thought.* Princeton: Princeton University Press.

Skidelsky, R. (2000). *John Maynard Keynes: Fighting for Freedom, 1937–1946.* New York: Penguin.

Solimano, A., ed. (2006). *Vanishing Growth in Latin America.* Northampton, Mass.: Edward Elgar.

Sridharan, E. (1996). *The Political Economy of Industrial Promotion: Indian, Brazilian, and Korean Electronics in Comparative Perspective, 1969–1994.* Westport, Conn.: Praeger.

Thorne, C. (1985). *The Issue of War: States, Societies, and the Far Eastern Conflict of 1941–1945.* New York: Oxford University Press.

Tignor, R. L. (1998). *Capitalism and Nationalism at the End of Empire: State and Business in Decolonizing Egypt, Nigeria, and Kenya, 1945–1963.* Princeton: Princeton University Press.

Tortella, G., ed. (1990). *Education and Economic Development since the Industrial Revolution.* Valencia: Generalitat Valenciana.

Toynbee, A. J. (1934–1961). *A Study of History.* 12 vols. London: Oxford University Press.

Tripathi, D., and M. Mehta (1990). *Business Houses in Western India: A Study of Entrepreneurial Responses, 1850–1956.* Columbia, Mo.: South Asia Publications.

Türkiye Is Bankasi A.S. (1967). *Development Plan of Turkey, Second Five-Year (1968–1972).* Ankara: Economic Research Department, Türkiye Is Bankasi A.S.

United Nations (2002). *Human Development Report 2002.* New York: Oxford University Press.

United Nations (various years). *World Investment Report.* Geneva: United Nations.

United Nations Conference on Trade and Development (various years). *Handbook of International Trade and Development Statistics.* Geneva: United Nations Conference on Trade and Development.

United States Trade Representative (1998). *Trade Policy Agenda and . . . Annual Report.* Washington, D.C.: Office of the United States Trade Representative.

Wade, R. (1990). *Governing the Market: Economic Theory and the Role of the Government in East Asian Industrialization.* Princeton: Princeton University Press.

Wilkins, M. (1974). *The Maturing of Multinational Enterprise: American Business Abroad from 1914 to 1970.* Cambridge: Harvard University Press.

Willis, E. J. (1990). *The Politicized Bureaucracy: Regimes, Presidents and Economic Policy in Brazil*. Boston: Boston College.

World Bank (various years). *World Development Report,* Development Indicators. Washington, D.C.: World Bank.

World Bank (1980, 1994). *World Tables*. Washington, D.C.: World Bank.

World Bank (1990). *World Development Report, Poverty*. Washington, D.C.: World Bank.

World Bank (1993). *The East Asian Miracle: Economic Growth and Public Policy*. New York: Oxford University Press.

Wurfel, D. (1988). *Filipino Politics: Development and Decay*. Ithaca: Cornell University Press.

Yonekura, S. (1994). *The Japanese Iron and Steel Industry, 1850–1990*. New York: St. Martin's.

Zaidi, S. A. (1999). *Issues in Pakistan's Economy*. Oxford: Oxford University Press.

Index